A PLAY BY
TOMSON HIGHWAY

Dry Lips
Oughta Move To
Kapuskasing

A PLAY BY TOMSON HIGHWAY

Dry Lips Oughta Move To Kapuskasing

FIFTH
HOUSE
PUBLISHERS

Published in Canada by Fifth House Ltd.
195 Allstate Parkway
Markham, ON L3R 4T8
www.fifthhousepublishers.ca

Published in the United States by Fifth House Ltd.
311 Washington Street, Brighton, Massachusetts 02135

Songs: "Generation," lyrics by Buffy Sainte-Marie. © 1972 Caleb Music. All rights reserved. Used by permission. "It Wasn't God Who Made Honky Tonk Angels" by J.D. Miller. Used by permission Peer Music Canada © 1952 by Peer International Corporation.

Library and Archives Canada Cataloguing in Publication
Highway, Tomson, 1951-
Dry lips oughta move to Kapuskasing : a play / by Tomson Highway.
Winner of the Dora Mavor Moore Award for Best New Play and nominated for the Governor General's Award.
ISBN 978-1-897252-83-3
I. Title.
PS8565.I433D7 2010 C812'.54 C2010-907648-6

United States Cataloguing-in-Publication Data is available from the Library of Congress

Fifth House Ltd. acknowledges with thanks the Canada Council for the Arts, and the Ontario Arts Council for their support of our publishing program. We acknowledge the financial support of the Government of Canada through the Canada Book Fund (CBF) for our publishing activities.

 ONTARIO ARTS COUNCIL
CONSEIL DES ARTS DE L'ONTARIO
an Ontario government agency
un organisme du gouvernement de l'Ontario

 Canada Council
for the Arts
Conseil des Arts
du Canada

Cover Design: BookWorks. Text Design: Media Clones Inc.
Printed and bound in Canada
14/21

Keetha kichi ooma masinaygun, Papa.
For my father, Joe Highway (1908–1988)

"...before the healing can take place,
the poison must first be exposed..."
Lyle Longclaws

Acknowledgments

Dry Lips Oughta Move to Kapuskasing premiered at Theatre Passe Muraille in Toronto on April 21, 1989, produced by Theatre Passe Muraille and Native Earth Performing Arts Inc., with the following cast:

Nanabush (as the spirit of Gazelle Nataways, Patsy Pegahmagahbow and Black Lady Halked) *Doris Linklater*
Zachary Jeremiah Keechigeesik *Gary Farmer*
Big Joey *Ben Cardinal*
Creature Nataways *Errol Kinistino*
Dickie Bird Halked *Kennetch Charlette*
Pierre St. Pierre *Graham Greene*
Spooky Lacroix *Ron Cook*
Simon Starblanket *Billy Merasty*
Hera Keechigeesik *Doris Linklater*

Directed by *Larry Lewis*
Set and costume design by *Brian Perchaluk*
Lighting design by *Stephan Droege*
Music by (and performed by) *Carlos Del Junco*
Choreography by *Rene Highway*
Stage Manager *Hilary Blackmore*
Production Manager *David Othen*

The author wishes to extend his deep gratitude to all the above as well as to the Prairie Theatre Exchange (Winnineg), which provided initial development funds for the writing of this play and to Playwrights' Workshop Montreal, where it was first workshopped. Finally, sincere thanks to all those others who helped make the first production of this play a dream come true: Elaine Bomberry, Tracy Bomberry, Gloria Eshkibok, Alan Generoux, Alun Hibbert, Max Ireland, Amos Keye, Raymond Lalonde, Paul Ledoux, the Native Canadian Centre of Toronto, The Honourable Gerry Phillips (Ontario Minister of Citizenship), Brian Richmond, Mike Sandy and, most especially, to the grandparents (Rita and Peter Bomberry) and the parents (Nancy Bomberry and Jim Kewakundo) of Sean Peter Kewakundo — and to Sean Peter Kewakundo himself — for providing the final, miraculous surprise of the show each night: Sean Peter Kewakundo, at the age of five months, played the baby of Zachary Jeremiah and Hera Keechigeesik during the last four minutes of *Dry Lips Oughta Move to Kapuskasing*.

Production Notes

The set for the original production of *Dry Lips Oughta Move to Kapuskasing* contained certain elements which I think are essential to the play.

First of all, it was designed on two levels, the lower of which was the domain of the "real" Wasaychigan Hill. This lower level contained, on stage-left, Big Joey's living room/kitchen, with its kitchen counter at the back and, facing down-stage, an old brown couch with a television set a few feet in front of it. This television set could be made to double as a smaller rock for the forest scenes. Stage-right had Spooky Lacroix's kitchen, with its kitchen counter (for which Big Joey's kitchen counter could double) and its table and chairs.

In front of all this was an open area, the floor of which was covered with teflon, a material which looks like ice and on which one can actually skate, using real ice skates; this was the rink for the hockey arena scenes. With lighting effects, this area could also be turned into "the forest" surrounding the village of Wasaychigan Hill, with its leafless winter trees. The only other essential element here was a larger jutting rock beside which, for instance, Zachary Jeremiah Keechigeesik and Simon Starblanket meet, a rock which could be made to glow at certain key points. Pierre's "little boot-leg joint" in Act Two, with its "window," was also created with lighting effects.

The upper level of the set was almost exclusively the realm of Nanabush. The principal element here was her perch, located in the very middle of this area. The perch was actually an old jukebox of a late 60's/early 70's make, but it was semi-hidden throughout most of the play, so that is was fully revealed as this fabulous jukebox only at those few times when it was needed; the effect sought after here is of this magical, mystical jukebox hanging in the night air, like a haunting and persistent memory, high up over the village of Wasaychigan Hill. Over and behind this perch was suspended a huge full moon whose glow came on, for the most part, only during the outdoor scenes, which all take place at nighttime. All other effects in this area were accomplished with lighting. The very front of this level, all along its edge, was also utilized as the "bleachers" area for the hockey arena scenes.

Easy access was provided for between the lower and the upper levels of this set.

The "sound-scape" of *Dry Lips Oughta Move to Kapuskasing* was mostly provided for by a musician playing, live, on harmonica, off to the side. It is as though the "dream-scape" of the play were laced all the way through with Zachary Jeremiah Keechigeesik's "idealized" form of harmonica playing, permeated with a definite "blues" flavor. Although Zachary ideally should play his harmonica, and not too well, in those few scenes where it is called for, the sound of this harmonica is most effectively used to under-line and highlight the many magical appearances of Nanabush in her various guises.

Spooky Lacroix's baby, towards the end of Act Two, can, and should, be played by a doll wrapped in a blanket. But for greatest effect, Zachary's baby, at the very end of the play, should be played by a real baby, preferably about five months of age.

Finally, both Cree and Ojibway are used freely in this text for the reasons that these two languages, belonging to the same linguistic family, are very similar and that the fictional reserve of Wasaychigan Hill has a mixture of both Cree and Ojibway residents.

Note: Words and passages in Cree and Ojibway are translated in parentheses, except as noted.

A Note On Nanabush

The dream world of North American Indian mythology is inhabited by the most fantastic creatures, beings and events. Foremost among these beings is the "Trickster," as pivotal and important a figure in our world as Christ is in the realm of Christian mythology. "Weesageechak" in Cree, "Nanabush" in Ojibway, "Raven" in others, "Coyote" in still others, this Trickster goes by many names and many guises. In fact, he can assume any guise he chooses. Essentially a comic, clownish sort of character, his role is to teach us about the nature and the meaning of existence on the planet Earth; he straddles the consciousness of man and that of God, the Great Spirit.

The most explicit distinguishing feature between the North American Indian languages and the European languages is that in Indian (e.g. Cree, Ojibway), there is no gender. In Cree, Ojibway, etc., unlike English, French, German, etc., the male-female-neuter hierarchy is entirely absent. So that by this system of thought, the central hero figure from our mythology — theology, if you will — is theoretically neither exclusively male nor exclusively female, or is both simultaneously. Therefore, where in *The Rez Sisters*, Nanabush was male, in this play — "flip-side" to *The Rez Sisters* — Nanabush is female.

Some say that Nanabush left this continent when the white man came. We believe she/he is still here among us — albeit a little the worse for wear and tear — having assumed other guises. Without the continued presence of this extraordinary figure, the core of Indian culture would be gone forever.

Cast Of Characters

(in order of appearance):

Nanabush (as the spirit of Gazelle Nataways, Patsy Pegahmagahbow and Black Lady Halked)
Zachary Jeremiah Keechigeesik* - 41 years old
Big Joey - 39
Creature Nataways - 39
Dickie Bird Halked - 17
Pierre St. Pierre - 53
Spooky Lacroix - 39
Simon Starblanket - 20
Hera Keechigeesik - 39

TIME:

Between Saturday, February 3, 1990, 11 p.m., and Saturday, February 10, 1990, 11 a.m.

PLACE:

The Wasaychigan** Hill Indian Reserve, Manitoulin Island, Ontario

NOTES:

*"Keechigeesik" means "heaven" or "great sky" in Cree.
**"Wasaychigan" means "window" in Ojibway.

Act One

The set for this first scene is the rather shabby and very messy living room/kitchen of the reserve house Big Joey and Gazelle Nataways currently share. Prominently displayed on one wall is a life-size pin-up poster of Marilyn Monroe. The remains of a party are obvious. On the worn-out old brown couch, with its back towards the entrance, lies Zachary Jeremiah Keechigeesik, a very handsome Indian man. He is naked, passed out. The first thing we see when the light comes up — a very small "spot," precisely focussed — is Zachary's bare, naked bum. Then, from behind the couch, we see a woman's leg, sliding languorously into a nylon stocking and right over Zachary's bum. It is Nanabush, as the spirit of Gazelle Nataways, dressing to leave. She eases herself luxuriously over the couch and over Zachary's bum and then reaches under Zachary's sleeping head, from where she gently pulls a gigantic pair of false, rubberized breasts. She proceeds to put these on over her own bare breasts. Then Nanabush/Gazelle Nataways sashays over to the side of the couch, picks a giant hockey sweater up off the floor and shimmies into it. The sweater has a huge, plunging neck-line, with the capital letter "W" and the number "1" prominently sewn on. Then she sashays back to the couch and behind it. Pleasurably and mischieviously, she leans over and plants a kiss on Zachary's bum, leaving behind a gorgeous, luminescent lip-stick mark. The last thing she does before she leaves is to turn the television on. This television sits facing the couch that Zachary lies on. Nanabush/Gazelle does not use her hand for this, though; instead, she turns the appliance on with one last bump of her voluptuous hips. "Hockey Night in Canada" comes on. The sound of this hockey game is on only slightly, so that we hear it as background "music" all the way through the coming scene. Then Nanabush/Gazelle exits, to sit on her perch on the upper level of the set. The only light left on stage is that coming from the television screen, giving off its eery glow. Beat.

The kitchen door bangs open, the "kitchen light" flashes on and Big Joey and Creature Nataways enter, Creature carrying a case of beer on his head. At first, they are oblivious to Zachary's presence. Also at about this time, the face of Dickie Bird Halked emerges from the shadows at the "kitchen window." Silently, he watches the rest of the proceedings, taking a particular interest — even fascination — in the movements and behavior of Big Joey.

BIG JOEY:

Calling out for Gazelle who, of course, is not home.
Hey, bitch!

CREATURE:

As he, at regular intervals, bangs the beer case down on the kitchen counter, rips it open, pops bottles open, throws one to Big Joey, all noises that serve to "punctuate" the rat-a-tat rhythm of his frenetic speech.
Batman oughta move to Kapuskasing, nah, Kap's too

good for Batman, right, Big Joey? I tole you once I tole you twice he shouldna done it he shouldna done what he went and did goddawful Batman Manitowabi the way he went and crossed that blue line with the puck, man, he's got the flippin' puck right in the palm of his flippin' hand and only a minute-and-a-half to go he just about gave me the shits the way Batman Manitowabi went and crossed that blue line right in front of that brick shithouse of a whiteman why the hell did that brick shithouse of a whiteman have to be there...

ZACHARY:
Talking in his sleep.
No!

CREATURE:
Hey!
Big Joey raises a finger signaling Creature to shut up.

ZACHARY:
I said no!

CREATURE:
In a hoarse whisper.
That's not a TV kind of sound.

BIG JOEY:
Shhh!

ZACHARY:
...goodness sakes, Hera, you just had a baby...

CREATURE:
That's a real life kind of sound, right, Big Joey?
Big Joey and Creature slowly come over to the couch.

ZACHARY:
...women playing hockey...damn silliest thing I heard in my life...

BIG JOEY:
Well, well...

CREATURE:

Ho-leee!

Whispering.

Hey, what's that on his arse look like lip marks.

ZACHARY:

...Simon Starblanket, that's who's gonna help me with my bakery...

CREATURE:

He's stitchless, he's nude, he's gonna pneumonia...

BIG JOEY:

Shut up.

CREATURE:

Get the camera. Chris'sakes, take a picture.

Creature scrambles for the Polaroid, which he finds under one end of the couch.

ZACHARY:

...Simon!

Jumps up.

What the?!

CREATURE:

Surprise!

Camera flashes.

ZACHARY:

Put that damn thing away. What are you doing here? Where's my wife? Hera!

He realizes he's naked, grabs a cast iron frying pan and slaps it over his crotch, almost castrating himself in the process.

Ooof!

BIG JOEY:

Smiling.

Over easy or sunny side up, Zachary Jeremiah Keechigee-sik?

ZACHARY:
Get outa my house.
CREATURE:
This ain't your house. This is Big Joey's house, right,
Big Joey?
BIG JOEY:
Shut up.
ZACHARY:
Creature Nataways. Get outa here. Gimme that
camera.
CREATURE:
Come and geeeet it!
Grabs Zachary's pants from the floor.
ZACHARY:
Cut it out. Gimme them goddamn pants.
CREATURE:
Singing.
Lipstick on your arshole, tole da tale on you-hoo.
ZACHARY:
What?
Straining to see his bum.
Oh lordy, lordy, lordy gimme them pants.
As he tries to wipe the stain off.
CREATURE:
Here doggy, doggy. Here poochie, poochie woof woof!
*Zachary grabs the pants. They rip almost completely
in half. Creature yelps.*
Yip!
*Momentary light up on Nanabush/Gazelle, up on her
perch, as she gives a throaty laugh. Big Joey echoes
this, Creature tittering away in the background.*
ZACHARY:
Hey, this is not my doing, Big Joey.
·*As he clumsily puts on what's left of his pants.*

Creature manages to get in one more shot with the camera.

We were just having a nice quiet drink over at Andy Manigitogan's when Gazelle Nataways shows up. She brought me over here to give me the recipe for her bannock apple pie cuz, goodness sakes, Simon Starblanket was saying it's the best, that pie was selling like hot cakes at the bingo and he knows I'm tryna establish this reserve's first pie-making business gimme that camera.

Big Joey suddenly makes a lunge at Zachary but Zachary evades him.

CREATURE:

In the background, like a little dog.

Yah, yah.

BIG JOEY:

Slowly stalking Zachary around the room.

You know, Zach, there's a whole lotta guys on this rez been slippin' my old lady the goods but there ain't but a handful been stupid enough to get caught by me.

He snaps his fingers and, as always, Creature obediently scurries over. He hands Big Joey the picture of Zachary naked on the couch. Big Joey shows the picture to Zachary, right up to his face.

Kinda em-bare-ass-in' for a hoity-toity educated community pillar like you, eh Zach?

Zachary grabs for the picture but Big Joey snaps it away.

ZACHARY:

What do you want?

BIG JOEY:

What's this I hear about you tellin' the chief I can wait for my radio station?

ZACHARY:

As he proceeds with looking around the room to collect and put on what he can find of his clothes. Big Joey and Creature follow him around, obviously enjoying his predicament.

I don't know where the hell you heard that from.

BIG JOEY:

Yeah, right. Well, Lorraine Manigitogan had a word or two with Gazelle Nataways the other night. When you presented your initial proposal at the band office, you said: "Joe can wait. He's only got another three months left in the hockey season."

ZACHARY:

I never said no such thing.

BIG JOEY:

Bull shit.

ZACHARY:

W-w-w-what I said was that employment at this bakery of mine would do nothing but add to those in such places as those down at the arena. I never mentioned your name once. And I said it only in passing reference to the fact...

BIG JOEY:

...that this radio idea of mine doesn't have as much long-term significance to the future of this community as this fancy bakery idea of yours, Mr. Pillsbury dough-boy, right?

ZACHARY:

If that's what you heard, then you didn't hear it from Lorraine Manigitogan. You got it from Gazelle Nataways and you know yourself she's got a bone to pick with...

BIG JOEY:
You know, Zach, you and me, we work for the same cause, don't we?

ZACHARY:
Never said otherwise.

BIG JOEY:
We work for the betterment and the advancement of this community, don't we? And seeing as we're about the only two guys in this whole hell-hole who's got the get-up-and-go to do something...

ZACHARY:
That's not exactly true, Joe. Take a look at Simon Starblanket...

BIG JOEY:
...we should be working together, not against. What do you say you simply postpone that proposal to the Band Council...

ZACHARY:
I'm sorry. Can't do that.

BIG JOEY:
Cornering Zachary.
Listen here, bud. You turned your back on me when everybody said I was responsible for that business in Espanola seventeen years ago and you said nothin'. I over-looked that. Never said nothin'.
Zachary remembers his undershorts and proceeds, with even greater desperation, to look for them, zeroing in on the couch and under it. Big Joey catches the drift and snaps his fingers, signaling Creature to look for the shorts under the couch. Creature jumps for the couch. Without missing a beat, Big Joey continues.
You turned your back on me when you said you didn't want nothin' to do with me from that day on. I over-

looked that. Never said nothin'. You gave me one hell
of a slap in the face when your wife gave my Gazelle
that kick in the belly. I overlooked that. Never said
nothin'.

*Creature, having found the shorts among the junk
under the couch just split seconds before Zachary
does, throws them to Big Joey. Big Joey holds the
shorts up to Zachary, smiling with satisfaction.*

That, however, was the last time...

ZACHARY:
That wasn't my fault, Joe. It's that witch woman of
yours Gazelle Nataways provoked that fight between
her and Hera and you know yourself Hera tried to come
and sew up her belly again...

BIG JOEY:
Zach. I got ambition...

ZACHARY:
Yeah, right.

BIG JOEY:
I aim to get that radio station off the ground, starting
with them games down at my arena.

ZACHARY:
Phhhh!

BIG JOEY:
I aim to get a chain of them community radio stations
not only on this here island but beyond as well...

ZACHARY:
Dream on, Big Joey, dream on...

BIG JOEY:
...and I aim to prove this broadcasting of games among
the folks is one sure way to get some pride...

ZACHARY:
Bullshit! You're in it for yourself.

BIG JOEY:

...some pride and dignity back so you just get your ass on out of my house and you go tell that Chief your Band Council Resolution can wait until next fiscal year or else...

ZACHARY:

I ain't doing no such thing, Joe, no way. Not when I'm this close.

BIG JOEY:

As he eases himself down onto the couch, twirling the shorts with his fore-finger.

...or else I get my Gazelle Nataways to wash these skivvies of yours, put them in a box all nice and gussied up, your picture on top, show up at your door-step and hand them over to your wife.

Silence.

ZACHARY:

Quietly, to Big Joey.

Gimme them shorts.

No answer. Then to Creature.

Gimme them snapshots.

Still no response.

BIG JOEY:

Dead calm.

Get out.

ZACHARY:

Seeing he can't win for the moment, prepares to exit.

You may have won this time, Joe, but...

BIG JOEY:

Like a steel trap.

Get out.

Silence. Finally Zachary exits, looking very humble. Seconds before Zachary's exit, Dicky Bird Halked, to avoid being seen by Zachary, disappears from the "window." The moment Zachary is gone, Creature scurries to the kitchen door, shaking his fist in the direction of the already-departed Zachary.

CREATURE:

Damn rights!

Then strutting like a cock, he turns to Big Joey.

Zachary Jeremiah Keechigeesik never shoulda come in your house, Big Joey. Thank god, Gazelle Nataways ain't my wife no more...

Big Joey merely has to throw a glance in Creature's direction to intimidate him. At once, Creature reverts back to his usual nervous self.

...not really, she's yours now, right, Big Joey? It's you she's livin' with these days, not me.

BIG JOEY:

As he sits on the couch with his beer, mostly ignoring Creature and watching the hockey game on television.

Don't make her my wife.

CREATURE:

But you live together, you sleep together, you eat ooops!

BIG JOEY:

Still don't make her my wife.

CREATURE:

As he proceeds to try to clean up the mess around the couch, mostly shoving everything back under it.

I don't mind, Big Joey, I really don't. I tole you once I tole you twice she's yours now. It's like I loaned her to you, I don't mind. I can take it. We made a deal, remember? The night she threw the toaster at me and just about broke my skull, she tole me: "I had enough, Creature Nataways, I had enough from you. I had your kids and I had your disease and that's all I ever want

from you, I'm leavin'." And then she grabbed her
suitcase and she grabbed the kids, no, she didn't even
grab the kids, she grabbed the TV and she just sashayed
herself over here. She left me. It's been four years now,
Big Joey, I know, I know. Oh, it was hell, it was hell
at first but you and me we're buddies since we're
babies, right? So I thought it over for about a year...then
one day I swallowed my pride and I got up off that
chesterfield and I walked over here, I opened your door
and I shook your hand and I said: "It's okay, Big Joey,
it's okay." And then we went and played darts in
Espanola except we kinda got side-tracked, remember,
Big Joey, we ended up on that three-day bender?

BIG JOEY:
Creature Nataways?

CREATURE:
What?

BIG JOEY:
You talk too much.

CREATURE:
I tole you once I tole you twice I don't mind...
But Pierre St. Pierre comes bursting in, in a state of
great excitement.

PIERRE:
Addressing the case of beer directly.
Hallelujah! Have you heard the news?

CREATURE:
Pierre St. Pierre. Chris'sakes, knock. You're walkin'
into a civilized house.

PIERRE:
The news. Have you heard the news?

CREATURE:
I'll tell you a piece of news. Anyways, we come in the
door and guess who...

BIG JOEY:
> *To Creature.*
> Sit down.

PIERRE:
> Gimme a beer.

CREATURE:
> *To Pierre.*
> Sit down.

PIERRE:
> Gimme a beer.

BIG JOEY:
> Give him a fuckin' beer.
> *But Pierre has already grabbed, opened and is drinking a beer.*

CREATURE:
> Have a beer.

PIERRE:
> *Talking out the side of his mouth, as he continues drinking.*
> Tank you.

BIG JOEY:
> Talk.

PIERRE:
> *Putting his emptied bottle down triumphantly and grabbing another beer.*
> Toast me.

BIG JOEY:
> Spit it out.

CREATURE:
> Chris' sakes.

PIERRE:
> Toast me.

CREATURE:
> Toast you? The hell for?

PIERRE:
Shut up. Just toast me.

CREATURE/BIG JOEY:
Toast.

PIERRE:
Tank you. You just toasted "The Ref."

CREATURE:
To Pierre.
The ref?
To Big Joey.
The what?

PIERRE:
"The Ref!"

CREATURE:
The ref of the what?

PIERRE:
The ref. I'm gonna be the referee down at the arena. Big Joey's arena. The Wasaychigan Hill Hippodrome.

CREATURE:
We already got a referee.

PIERRE:
Yeah, but this here's different, this here's special.

BIG JOEY:
I'd never hire a toothless old bootlegger like you.

PIERRE:
They play their first game in just a coupla days. Against the Canoe Lake Bravettes. And I got six teeth left so you just keep you trap shut about my teeth.

CREATURE:
The Canoe Lake Bravettes?

BIG JOEY:
Who's "they?"

PIERRE:
Haven't you heard?

BIG JOEY:
Who's "they?"
PIERRE:
I don't believe this.
BIG JOEY:
Who's "they?"
PIERRE:
I don't believe this.
Big Joey bangs Pierre on the head.
Oww, you big bully! The Wasaychigan Hill Wailer-
ettes, of course. I'm talkin' about the Wasy Wailer-
ettes, who else geez.
CREATURE:
The Wasy Wailerettes? Chris' sakes...
PIERRE:
Dominique Ladouche, Black Lady Halked, that ter-
rible Dictionary woman, Fluffy Sainte-Marie, Dry Lips
Manigitogan, Leonarda Lee Starblanket, Annie Cook,
June Bug McLeod, Big Bum Pegahmagahbow, all twenty-
seven of 'em. Them women from right here on this
reserve, a whole batch of 'em, they upped and they said:
"Bullshit! Ain't nobody on the face of this earth's
gonna tell us us women's got no business playin'
hockey. That's bullshit!" That's what they said:
"Bullshit!" So. They took matter into their own
hands. And, holy shit la marde, I almost forgot to tell
you my wife Veronique St. Pierre, she went and made
up her mind she's joinin' the Wasy Wailerettes, only
the other women wouldn't let her at first on account
she never had no babies — cuz, you see, you gotta be
pregnant or have piles and piles of babies to be a Wasy
Wailerette — but my wife, she put her foot down and
she says: "Zhaboonigan Peterson may be just my
adopted daughter and she may be retarded as a doormat

but she's still my baby." That's what she says to 'em.
And she's on and they're playin' hockey and the Wasy
Wailerettes, they're just a-rarin' to go, who woulda
thunk it, huh?

CREATURE:
Ho-leee!

PIERRE:
God's truth...

BIG JOEY:
They never booked the ice.

PIERRE:
Ha! Booked it through Gazelle Nataways. Sure as I'm
alive and walkin' these treacherous icy roads...

BIG JOEY:
Hang on.

PIERRE:
...god's truth in all its naked splendor.
As he pops open yet another beer.
I kid you not, gentlemen, not for one slippery goddamn
minute. Toast!

BIG JOEY:
Grabbing the bottle right out of Pierre's mouth.
Where'd you sniff out all this crap?

PIERRE:
From my wife, who else? My wife, Veronique St.
Pierre, she told me. She says to me: "Pierre St. Pierre,
you'll eat your shorts but I'm playin' hockey and I don't
care what you say. Or think." And she left. No. First,
she cleaned out my wallet,
Grabs his beer back from Big Joey's hand.
grabbed her big brown rosaries from off the wall. Then
she left. Just slammed the door and left. Period. I just
about ate my shorts. Toast!

CREATURE:
Shouldn't we...shouldn't we stop them?

PIERRE:
Phhht!...

Creature just misses getting spat on.

CREATURE:
Ayoah!

PIERRE:
...Haven't seen hide nor hair of 'em since. Gone to Sudbury. Every single last one of 'em. Piled theirselves into seven cars and just took off. Them back wheels was squealin' and rattlin' like them little jinger bells. Just past tea-time. Shoppin'. Hockey equipment. Phhht!

Again, Creature just misses getting spat on.

CREATURE:
Ayoah! It's enough to give you the shits every time he opens his mouth.

PIERRE:
And they picked me. Referee.

BIG JOEY:
And why you, may I ask?

PIERRE:
Faking humility.
Oh, I don't know. Somethin' about the referee here's too damn perschnickety. That drum-bangin' young whipperschnapper, Simon Starblanket,
Grabbing yet another beer.
he's got the rules all mixed up or somethin' like that, is what they says. They kinda wanna play it their own way. So they picked me. Toast me.

CREATURE:
Toast.

PIERRE:
To the ref.
CREATURE:
To the ref.
PIERRE:
Tank you.
They both drink.
Ahhh.
Pause. To Big Joey.
So. I want my skates.
CREATURE:
Your skates?
PIERRE:
My skates. I want 'em back.
CREATURE:
The hell's he talkin' about now?
PIERRE:
They're here. I know they're here. I loaned 'em to you,
remember?
BIG JOEY:
Run that by me again?
PIERRE:
I loaned 'em to you. That Saturday night Gazelle Na-
taways came in that door with her TV and her suitcase
and you and me we were sittin' right there on that old
chesterfield with Lalala Lacroix sittin' between us and
I loaned you my skates in return for that forty-ouncer
of rye and Gazelle Nataways plunked her TV down,
marched right up to Lalala Lacroix, slapped her in the
face and chased her out the door. But we still had time
to make the deal whereby if I wanted my skates back
you'd give 'em back to me if I gave you back your forty-
ouncer, right? Right.
Produces the bottle from under his coat.
Ta-da! Gimme my skates.

BIG JOEY:
You sold them skates. They're mine.
PIERRE:
Never you mind, Big Joey, never you mind. I want my skates. Take this. Go on. Take it.
Big Joey fishes one skate out from under the couch.
CREATURE:
To himself, as he sits on the couch.
Women playin' hockey. Ho-leee!
Big Joey and Pierre exchange bottle and skate.
PIERRE:
Tank you.
He makes a triumphant exit. Big Joey merely sits there and waits knowingly. Silence. Then Pierre suddenly re-enters.
There's only one.
Silence.
Well, where the hell's the other one?
Silence. Pierre nearly explodes with indignation.
Gimme back my bottle! Where's the other one?
BIG JOEY:
You got your skate. I got my bottle.
PIERRE:
Don't talk backwards at me. I'm your elder.
CREATURE:
It's gone.
PIERRE:
Huh?
CREATURE:
Gone. The other skate's gone, right, Big Joey?
PIERRE:
Gone? Where?
CREATURE:
My wife Gazelle Nataways...

PIERRE:
...your ex-wife...

CREATURE:
...she threw it out the door two years ago the night Spooky Lacroix went crazy in the head and tried to come and rip Gazelle Nataways' door off for cheatin' at the bingo. Just about killed Spooky Lacroix too, right, Big Joey?

PIERRE:
So where's my other skate?

CREATURE:
At Spooky Lacroix's, I guess.

PIERRE:
Aw, shit la marde, you'se guys don't play fair.

BIG JOEY:
You go over to Spooky Lacroix's and you tell him I told you you could have your skate back.

PIERRE:
No way, José. Spooky Lacroix's gonna preach at me.

BIG JOEY:
Preach back.

PIERRE:
You come with me. You used to be friends with Spooky Lacroix. You talk to Spooky Lacroix. Spooky Lacroix likes you.

BIG JOEY:
He likes you too.

PIERRE:
Yeah, but he likes you better. Oh, shit la marde!
As he takes another beer out of the case.
And I almost forgot to tell you they decided to make Gazelle Nataways captain of the Wasy Wailerettes. I mean, she kind of...decided on her own, if you know what I mean.

BIG JOEY:
Spooky Lacroix's waitin' for you.

PIERRE:
How do you know?

BIG JOEY:
God told me.

PIERRE:
Pause. Pierre actually wonders to himself. Then:
Aw, bullshit.
Exits. Silence. Then Big Joey and Creature look at each other, break down and laugh themselves into prolonged hysterical fits. After a while, they calm down and come to a dead stop. They sit and think. They look at the hockey game on the television. Then, dead serious, they turn to each other.

CREATURE:
Women...Gazelle Nataways...hockey? Ho-leee...

BIG JOEY:
Still holding Pierre's bottle of whiskey.
Chris'sakes...
Fade-out.

From this darkness emerges the sound of Spooky Lacroix's voice, singing with great emotion. As he sings, the lights fade in on his kitchen, where Dickie Bird Halked is sitting across the table from Spooky Lacroix. Dickie Bird is scribbling on a piece of paper with a pencil. Spooky is knitting (pale blue baby booties). A bible sits on the table to the left of Spooky, a knitting pattern to his right. The place is covered with knitted doodads: knitted doilies, tea cozy, a tacky picture of "The Last Supper" with knitted frame and, on the wall, as subtly conspicuous as possible, a crucifix with pale blue knitted baby boo-

ties covering each of its four extremities. Throughout this scene, Spooky periodically consults the knitting pattern, wearing tiny little reading glasses, perched "just so" on the end of his nose. He knits with great difficulty and, therefore, with great concentration, sometimes, in moments of excitement, getting the bible and the knitting pattern mixed up with each other. He has tremendous difficulty getting the "disturbed" Dickie Bird to sit still and pay attention.

SPOOKY:

Singing.

Everybody oughta know. Everybody oughta know. Who Jesus is.

Speaking.

This is it. This is the end. Igwani eeweepoonaskeewuk. ("The end of the world is at hand.") Says right here in the book. Very, very, very important to read the book. If you want the Lord to come into your life, Dickie Bird Halked, you've got to read the book. Not much time left. Yessiree. 1990. The last year. This will be the last year of our lives. Clear as a picture. The end of the world is here. At last. About time too, with the world going crazy, people shooting, killing each other left, right and center. Jet planes full of people crashing into the bushes, lakes turning black, fish choking to death. Terrible. Terrible.

Dickie Bird shoves a note he's been scribbling over to Spooky.

What's this?

Spooky reads, with some difficulty.

"How...do...you...make...babies?"

Shocked.

Dickie Bird Halked? At your age? Surely. Anyway. That young Starblanket boy who went and shot him-

self. Right here. Right in the einsteins. Bleeding from
the belly, all this white mushy stuff come oozing out.
Yuch! Brrr! I guess there's just nothing better to do for
the young people on this reserve these days than go
around shooting their einsteins out from inside their
bellies. But the Lord has had enough. He's sick of it.
No more, he says, no more. This is it.
*Dickie Bird shoves another note over. Spooky pauses
to read. And finishes.*
Why, me and Lalala, we're married. And we're gonna
have a baby. Period. Now. When the world comes to
an end? The sky will open up. The clouds will part.
And the Lord will come down in a holy vapor. And
only those who are born-again Christian will go with
him when he goes back up. And the rest? You know
what's gonna happen to the rest? They will die. Big
Joey, for instance, they will go to hell and they will
burn for their wicked, whorish ways. But we will be
taken up into the clouds to spend eternity surrounded
by the wondrous and the mystical glory of god. Clear
as a picture, Dickie Bird Halked, clear as a picture. So
I'm telling you right now, you've got to read the book.
Very, very, very important.
*Dickie Bird shoves a third note over to Spooky.
Spooky reads and finishes.*
Why, Wellington Halked's your father, Dickie Bird
Halked. Don't you be asking questions like that. My
sister, Black Lady Halked, that's your mother. Right?
And because Wellington Halked is married to Black
Lady Halked, he is your father. And don't you ever let
no one tell you different.
Black-out.

From the darkness of the theater emerges the magical flickering of a luminescent powwow dancing bustle. As it moves gradually towards the down-stage area, a second — and larger — bustle appears on the upper level of the set, also flickering magically and moving about. The two bustles "play" with each other, almost affectionately, looking like two giant fire flies. The smaller bustle finally reaches the downstage area and from behind it emerges the face of Simon Starblanket. He is dancing and chanting in a forest made of light and shadows. The larger bustle remains on the upper level; behind it is the entire person of Nanabush as the spirit of Patsy Pegahmagahbow, a vivacious young girl of eighteen with a very big bum (i.e., an over-sized prosthetic bum). From this level, Nanabush/Patsy watches and "plays" with the proceedings on the lower level. The giant full moon is in full bloom behind her. From the very beginning of all this, and in counterpoint to Simon's chanting, also emerges the sound of someone playing a harmonica, a sad, mournful tune. It is Zachary Jeremiah Keechigeesik, stuck in the bush in his embarrasing state, playing his heart out. Then the harmonica stops and, from the darkness, we hear Zachary's voice.

ZACHARY:
Hey.
Simon hears this, looks behind, but sees nothing and continues his chanting and dancing. Simon chants and dances as though he were desperately trying to find the right chant and dance. Then:
Pssst!

SIMON:
Awinuk awa? ("Who's this?")

ZACHARY:

In a hoarse whisper.

Simon Starblanket.

SIMON:

Neee*, Zachary Jeremiah Keechigeesik. Awus! ("Go away!") Katha peeweestatooweemin. ("Don't come bothering me [with your words].")

Finally, Zachary emerges from the shadows and from behind a large rock, carrying his harmonica in one hand and holding his torn pants together as best he can with the other. Simon ignores him and continues with his chanting and dancing.

ZACHARY:

W-w-w-what's it cost to get one of them dough-making machines?

SIMON:

Not quite believing his ears.

What?

ZACHARY:

Them dough-making machines. What's it cost to buy one of them?

SIMON:

A Hobart?

ZACHARY:

A what?

SIMON:

Hobart. H-O-B-A-R-T. Hobart.

ZACHARY:

To himself.

Hobart. Hmmm.

---

* "Neee" is probably the most common Cree expression, meaning something like "Oh, you" *or* "My goodness."

SIMON:

Amused at the rather funny-looking Zachary.

Neee, machi ma-a, ("Oh you, but naturally,") Westinghouse for refrigerators, Kellogg's for corn flakes igwa ("and") Hobart for dough-making machines. Kinsitootawin na? ("Get it?") Brand name. Except we used to call it "the pig" because it had this...piggish kind of motion to it. But never mind. Awus. Don't bother me.

ZACHARY:

What's it cost to get this...pig?

SIMON:

Laughing.

Neee, Zachary Jeremiah, here you are, one of Wasy's most respected citizens, standing in the middle of the bush on a Saturday night in February freezing your buns off and you want to know how much a pig costs?

ZACHARY:

Vehemently.

I promised Hera I'd have all this information by tonight we were supposed to sit down and discuss the budget for this damn bakery tonight and here I went and messed it all up thank god I ran into you because now you're the only person left on this whole reserve who might have the figures I need what's this damn dough-making machine cost come on now tell me!

SIMON:

A little cowed.

Neee, about four thousand bucks. Maybe five.

ZACHARY:

You don't know for sure? But you worked there.

SIMON:

I was only the dishwasher, Zachary Jeremiah, I didn't own the place. Mama Louisa was a poor woman. She had really old equipment, most of which she dragged over herself all the way from Italy after the Second World War. It wouldn't cost the same today.

ZACHARY:

Five thousand dollars for a Mobart, hmmm...

SIMON:

Hobart.

ZACHARY:

I wish I had a piece of paper to write all this down, sheesh. You got a piece of paper on you?

SIMON:

No. Just...this.

Holding the dancing bustle up.

Why are you holding yourself like that?

ZACHARY:

I was...standing on the road down by Andy Manigito-gan's place when this car came by and wooof! My pants ripped. Ripped right down the middle. And my shorts, well, they just...took off. How do you like that, eh?

SIMON:

Nope. I don't like it. Neee, awus. Kigithaskin. ("You're lying to me.")

ZACHARY:

W-w-w-why would I pull your leg for? I don't really mind it except it is damn cold out here.

At this point, Nanabush/Patsy, on the upper level, scurries closer to get a better look, her giant pow-wow dancing bustle flickering magically in the half-light. Simon's attention is momentarily pulled away by this fleeting vision.

SIMON:

Hey! Did you see that?

But Zachary, too caught up with his own dilemma, does not notice.

ZACHARY:
I'm very, very upset right now...

SIMON:
...I thought I just saw Patsy Pegahmagahbow...with this...

ZACHARY:
As he looks, perplexed, in the direction Simon indicates.
...do you think...my two ordinary convection ovens...

SIMON:
Calling out.
Patsy?...
Pause. Then, slowly, he turns back to Zachary.
...like...she made this for me, eh?
Referring to the bustle.
She and her step-mother, Rosie Kakapetum, back in September, after my mother's funeral. Well, I was out here thinking, if this... like, if this...dance didn't come to me real natural, like from deep inside of me, then I was gonna burn it.
Referring to the bustle.
Right here on this spot. Cuz then...it doesn't mean anything real to me, does it? Like, it's false...it's driving me crazy, this dream where Indian people are just dropping off like flies...
Nanabush/Patsy begins to "play" with the two men, almost as if with the help of the winter night's magic and the power of the full moon, she were weaving a spell around Simon and Zachary.

ZACHARY:
Singing softly to himself.
Hot cross buns. Hot cross buns. One a penny, two a penny, hot cross buns...

SIMON:

...something has to be done...

ZACHARY:

Speaking.

...strawberry pies...

SIMON:

...in this dream...

ZACHARY:

...so fresh and flakey they fairly bubble over with the cream from the very breast of Mother Nature herself...

SIMON:

...the drum has to come back, mistigwuskeek ("the drum")...

ZACHARY:

...bran muffins, cherry tarts...

SIMON:

...the medicine, the power, this...

Holding the bustle up in the air.

ZACHARY:

...butter tarts...

SIMON:

...has to come back. We've got to learn to dance again.

ZACHARY:

...tarts tarts tarts upside-down cakes cakes cakes and not to forget, no, never, ever to forget that Black Forest Cake...

SIMON:

...Patsy Pegahmagahbow...

ZACHARY:

...cherries jubilee...

SIMON:

...her step-mother, Rosie Kakapetum, the medicine woman...

ZACHARY:
...lemon meringue pie...
SIMON:
...the power...
ZACHARY:
...baked Alaska...
SIMON:
...Nanabush!...
ZACHARY:
Then suddenly, with bitterness.
...Gazelle Nataways. K'skanagoos! ("The female dog!")
All of a sudden, from the darkness of the winter night, emerges a strange, eery sound; whether it is wolves howling or women wailing, we are not sure at first. And whether this sound comes from somewhere deep in the forest, from the full moon or where, we are not certain. But there is definitely a "spirit" in the air. The sound of this wailing is under-cut by the sound of rocks hitting boards, or the sides of houses, echoing, as in a vast empty chamber. Gradually, as Simon speaks, Zachary — filled with confusing emotion as he is — takes out his harmonica, sits down on the large rock and begins to play, a sad, mournful melody, tinged, as always, with a touch of the blues.
SIMON:
...I have my arms around this rock, this large black rock sticking out of the ground, right here on this spot. And then I hear this baby crying, from inside this rock. The baby is crying out my name. As if I am somehow responsible for it being caught inside that rock. I can't move. My arms, my whole body, stuck to this rock. Then this...eagle...lands beside me, right over there. But this bird has three faces, three women. And the eagle says to me: "the baby is crying, my grand-child is

crying to hear the drum again."

Nanabush/Patsy, her face surrounded by the brilliant feathers of her bustle, so that she looks like some fantastic, mysterious bird, begins to wail, her voice weaving in and out of the other wailing voices.

There's this noise all around us, as if rocks are hitting the sides of houses — echoing and echoing like in a vast empty room — and women are wailing. The whole world is filled with this noise.

Then Simon, too, wails, a heart-searing wail. From here on, all the wailing begins to fade.

Then the eagle is gone and the rock cracks and this mass of flesh, covered with veins and blood, comes oozing out and a woman's voice somewhere is singing something about angels and god and angels and god...

The wailing has now faded into complete silence. Zachary finally rises from his seat on the rock.

ZACHARY:
... I dreamt I woke up at Gazelle Nataways' place with no shorts on. And I got this nagging suspicion them shorts are still over there. If you could just go on over there now... I couldn't have been over there. I mean, there's my wife Hera. And there's my bakery. And this bakery could do a lot for the Indian people. Economic development. Jobs. Bread. Apple pie. So you see, there's an awful lot that's hanging on them shorts. This is a good chance for you to do something for your people, Simon, if you know what I mean...

SIMON:
I'm the one who has to bring the drum back. And it's Patsy's medicine power, that stuff she's learning from her step-mother Rosie Kakapetum that...helps me...

ZACHARY:
I go walking into my house with no underwear, pants

ripped right down the middle, not a shred of budget in
sight and wooof!...

*Pierre St. Pierre comes bursting in on the two men
with his one skate in hand, taking them completely
by suprise. Nanabush/Patsy disappears.*

ZACHARY:

Pierre St. Pierre! Just the man...

PIERRE:

No time. No time. Lalala Lacroix's having a baby any
minute now so I gotta get over to Spook's before she
pops.

SIMON:

I can go get Rosie Kakapetum.

PIERRE:

Too old. Too old. She can't be on the team.

SIMON:

Neee, what team? Rosie Kakapetum's the last mid-
wife left in Wasy, Pierre St. Pierre, of course she can't
be on a team.

ZACHARY:

To Pierre.

You know that greasy shit-brown chesterfield over at
Gazelle Nataways?

SIMON:

To Zachary.

Mind you, if there was a team of mid-wives, chee-i?
("eh?") Wha!

PIERRE:

Gazelle Nataways? Hallelujah, haven't you heard the
news?

ZACHARY:

What?...you mean...it's out already?

PIERRE:

All up and down Wasaychigan Hill...

ZACHARY:
Thoughtfully, to himself, as it dawns on him.
The whole place knows.

PIERRE:
...clean across Manitoulin Island and right to the outskirts of Sudbury...

ZACHARY:
Lordy, lordy, lordy...

PIERRE:
Gazelle Nataways, Dominique Ladouche, Black Lady Halked, that terrible Dictionary woman, Fluffy Sainte-Marie, Dry Lips Manigitogan, Leonarda Lee Starblanket, Annie Cook, June Bug McLeod, Big Bum Pegahmagahbow...

SIMON:
Patsy Pegahmagahbow. Get it straight...

PIERRE:
Quiet! I'm not finished...all twenty-seven of 'em...

SIMON:
Neee, Zachary Jeremiah, your goose is cooked.

PIERRE:
Phhht! Cooked and burnt right down to a nice crispy pitch black cinder because your wife Hera Keechigeesik is in on it too.
Zachary, reeling from the horror of it all, finally sits back down on the rock.

SIMON:
Patsy Pegahmagahbow is pregnant, Pierre St. Pierre. She can't go running around all over Manitoulin Island with a belly that's getting bigger by the...

PIERRE:
Aw, they're all pregnant, them women, or have piles and piles of babies and I'll be right smack dab in the middle of it all just a-blowin' my whistle and a-throwin' that dirty little black thingie around...

ZACHARY:

Rising from the rock.

Now you listen here, Pierre St. Pierre. I may have lost my shorts under Gazelle Nataways' greasy shit-brown chesterfield not one hour ago and I may have lost my entire life, not to mention my bakery, as a result of that one very foolish mistake but I'll have you know that my shorts, they are clean as a whistle, I change them every day, my favorite color is light blue and black and crusted with shit my shorts most certainly are not!

SIMON:

Surprised and thrilled at Zachary's renewed "fighting" spirit.

Wha!

PIERRE:

Whoa! Easy, Zachary Jeremiah, easy there. Not one stitch of your shorts has anything whatsoever to do with the revolution.

SIMON:

Pierre St. Pierre, what revolution are you wheezing and snorting on about?

PIERRE:

The puck. I'm talkin' about the puck.

ZACHARY:

The puck?

SIMON:

The puck?

PIERRE:

Yes, the puck. The puck, the puck, the puck and nothin' but the goddam puck they're playin' hockey, them women from right here on this reserve, they're playin' hockey and nothin', includin' Zachary Jeremiah Keechigeesik's bright crispy undershorts, is gonna stop 'em.

SIMON:

Women playing hockey. Neee, watstagatch! ("Good grief!")

PIERRE:

"Neee, watstagatch" is right because they're in Sudbury, as I speak, shoppin' for hockey equipment, and I'm the referee! Outa my way! Or the Lacroixs will pop before I get there.

He begins to exit.

ZACHARY:

Pierre St. Pierre, get me my shorts or I'll report your bootleg joint to the police.

PIERRE:

No time. No time.

Exits.

ZACHARY:

Calling out.

Did Hera go to Sudbury, too?

But Pierre is gone.

SIMON:

Thoughtfully to himself, as he catches another glimpse of Nanabush/Patsy and her bustle.

...rocks hitting boards...

ZACHARY:

To himself.

What in God's name is happening to Wasaychigan Hill...

SIMON:

...women wailing...

ZACHARY:

With even greater urgency.

Do you think those two ordinary convection ovens are gonna do the job or should I get one of them great big pizza ovens right away?

SIMON:

...pucks...

ZACHARY:

Simon, I'm desperate!

SIMON:

Finally, snapping out of his speculation and looking straight into Zachary's face.

Neee, Zachary Jeremiah. Okay. Goes like this.

Then, very quickly:

It depends on what you're gonna bake, eh? Like if you're gonna bake bread and, like, lots of it, you're gonna need one of them great big ovens but if you're gonna bake just muffins...

ZACHARY:

In the background.

...muffins, nah, not just muffins...

SIMON:

...then all you need is one of them ordinary little ovens but like I say, I was only the dishwasher...

ZACHARY:

How many employees were there in your bakery?

SIMON:

...it depends on how big a community you're gonna serve, Zachary Jeremiah...

ZACHARY:

...nah, Wasy, just Wasy, to start with...

SIMON:

...like, we had five, one to make the dough — like, mix the flour and the water and the yeast and all that — like, this guy had to be at work by six a.m., that's gonna be hard here in Wasy, Zachary Jeremiah, I'm telling you that right now...

ZACHARY:

...nah, I can do that myself, no problem...

SIMON:

...then we had three others to roll the dough and knead and twist and punch and pound it on this great big wooden table...

ZACHARY:

...I'm gonna need a great big wooden table?...

SIMON:

...hard wood, Zachary Jeremiah, not soft wood. And then one to actually bake the loaves, like, we had these long wooden paddles, eh?...

ZACHARY:

...paddles...

SIMON:

...yeah, paddles, Zachary Jeremiah, real long ones. It was kinda neat, actually...

ZACHARY:

...go on, go on...

SIMON:

Listen here, Zachary Jeremiah, I'm going to Sudbury next Saturday, okay? And if you wanna come along, I can take you straight to Mama Louisa's Pasticerria myself. I'll introduce you to the crusty old girl and you can take a good long look at her rubbery old Hobart, how's that? You can even touch it if you want, neee...

ZACHARY:

...really?...

SIMON:

Me? I'm asking Patsy Pegahmagahbow to marry me...

ZACHARY:

...Simon, Simon...

SIMON:

...and we're gonna hang two thousand of these things *Referring to his dancing bustle.* all over Manitoulin Island, me and Patsy and our baby.

And me and Patsy and our baby and this Nanabush character, we're gonna be dancing up and down Wasaychigan Hill like nobody's business cuz I'm gonna go out there and I'm gonna bring that drum back if it kills me.

ZACHARY:

Pause. Then, quietly.

Get me a safety pin.

SIMON:

Pause.

Neee, okay. And you, Zachary Jeremiah Keechigeesik, you're gonna see a Hobart such as you have never seen ever before in your entire life!

SIMON/ZACHARY:

Smiling, almost laughing, at each other.

Neee...

Black-out.

Lights up on the upper level, where we see this bizarre vision of Nanabush, now in the guise of Black Lady Halked, nine months pregnant (i.e., wearing a huge, out-sized prosthetic belly). Over this, she wears a maternity gown and, pacing the floor slowly, holds a huge string of rosary beads. She recites the rosary quietly to herself. She is also drinking a beer and, obviously, is a little unsteady on her feet because of this.

Fade-in on the lower level into Spooky Lacroix's kitchen. Dickie Bird Halked is on his knees, praying fervently to this surrealistic, miraculous vision of "the Madonna" (i.e., his own mother), which he actually sees inside his own mind. Oblivious to all this, Spooky Lacroix sits at his table, still knitting his baby booties and preaching away.

SPOOKY:

Dickie Bird Halked? I want you to come to heaven with me. I insist. But before you do that, you take one of them courses in sign language, help me prepare this reserve for the Lord. Can't you just see yourself, standing on that podium in the Wasaychigan Hill Hippodrome, talking sign language to the people? Talking about the Lord and how close we are to the end? I could take a break. And these poor people with their meaningless, useless...

Pierre St. Pierre comes bursting in and marches right up to Spooky. The vision of Nanabush/Black Lady Halked disappears.

PIERRE:

Alright. Hand it over.

SPOOKY:

Startled out of his wits.

Pierre St. Pierre! You went and mixed up my booty!

PIERRE:

I know it's here somewhere.

SPOOKY:

Whatever it is you're looking for, you're not getting it until you bring the Lord into your life.

PIERRE:

My skate. Gimme my skate.

SPOOKY:

I don't have no skate. Now listen to me.

PIERRE:

My skate. The skate Gazelle Nataways threw at you and just about killed you.

SPOOKY:

What the hell are you gonna do with a skate at this hour of the night?

PIERRE:
Haven't you heard the news?

SPOOKY:
Pauses to think.
No. I haven't heard any news.
Dickie Bird gets up and starts to wander around the kitchen. He looks around at random, first out the window, as if to see who has been chanting, then, eventually, he zeroes in on the crucifix on the wall and stands there looking at it. Finally, he takes it off the wall and plays with its cute little booties.

PIERRE:
The women. I'm gonna be right smack dab in the middle of it all. The revolution. Right here in Wasaychigan Hill.

SPOOKY:
The Chief or the priest. Which one are they gonna revolution?

PIERRE:
No, no, no. Dominique Ladouche, Black Lady Halked, that terrible Dictionary woman, that witch Gazelle Nataways, Fluffy Sainte-Marie, Dry Lips Manigitogan, Leonarda Lee Starblanket, Annie Cook, June Bug McLeod, Big Bum Pegahmagahbow, all twenty-seven of 'em. Even my wife, Veronique St. Pierre, she'll be right smack dab in the middle of it all. Defense.

SPOOKY:
Defense? The Americans. We're being attacked. Is the situation that serious?

PIERRE:
No, no, no, for Chris' sakes. They're playin' hockey. Them women are playin' hockey. Dead serious they are too.

SPOOKY:

No.

PIERRE:

Yes.

SPOOKY:

Thank the Lord this is the last year!

PIERRE:

Don't you care to ask?

SPOOKY:

Thank the Lord the end of the world is coming this year!

Gasping, he marches up to Dickie Bird.

PIERRE:

I'm the referee, dammit.

SPOOKY:

Watch your language.

Grabbing the crucifix from Dickie Bird.

PIERRE:

That's what I mean when I say I'm gonna be right smack dab in the middle of it all. You don't listen to me.

SPOOKY:

As he proceeds to put the little booties back on the crucifix.

But you're not a woman.

PIERRE:

You don't have to be. To be a referee these days, you can be anything, man or woman, don't matter which away. So gimme my skate.

SPOOKY:

What skate?

PIERRE:

The skate Gazelle Nataways just about killed you with after the bingo that time.

SPOOKY:

Oh, that. I hid it in the basement.

Pierre opens a door, falls in and comes struggling out with a mouse trap stuck to a finger.

Pierre St. Pierre, what the hell are you doing in Lalala's closet?

PIERRE:

Well, where the hell's the basement?

He frees his finger.

SPOOKY:

Pierre St. Pierre, you drink too much. You gotta have the Lord in your life.

PIERRE:

I don't need the Lord in my life, for god's sake, I need my skate. I gotta practice my figure eights.

SPOOKY:

As he begins to put the crucifix back up on the wall.

You gotta promise me before I give you your skate.

PIERRE:

I promise.

SPOOKY:

Unaware, he threatens Pierre with the crucifix, holding it up against his neck.

You gotta have the Lord come into your life.

PIERRE:

Alright, alright.

SPOOKY:

For how long?

PIERRE:

My whole life. I promise I'm gonna bring the Lord into my life and keep him there right up until the day I die just gimme my goddamn skate.

SPOOKY:

Cross my heart.

PIERRE:

Alright? Cross your heart.

Neither man makes a move, until Spooky, finally catching on, throws Pierre a look. Pierre crosses himself.

SPOOKY:

Good.

Exits to the basement.

PIERRE:

Now alone with Dickie Bird, half-whispering to him. As Pierre speaks, Dickie Bird again takes the crucifix off the wall and returns with it to his seat and there takes the booties off in haphazard fashion.

Has he been feedin' you this crappola, too? Don't you be startin' that foolishness. That Spooky Lacroix's so fulla shit he wouldn't know a two thousand year-old Egyptian Sphinxter if he came face to face with one. He's just preachifyin' at you because you're the one person on this reserve who can't argue back. You listen to me. I was there in the same room as your mother when she gave birth to you. So I know well who you are and where you come from. I remember the whole picture. Even though we were all in a bit of a fizzy...I remember. Do you know, Dickie Bird Halked, that you were named after that bar? Anyone ever tell you that?

Dickie Bird starts to shake. Pierre takes fright.

Spooky Lacroix, move that holy ass of yours, for fuck's sakes!

Dickie Bird laughs. Pierre makes a weak attempt to laugh along.

And I'll never forgive your father, Big Joey oops...

Dickie Bird reacts.

...I mean, Wellington Halked, for letting your mother

do that to you. "Its not good for the people of this world," I says to him "it's not good for 'em to have the first thing they see when they come into the world is a goddamn jukebox." That's what I says to him. Thank god, you survived, Dickie Bird Halked, thank god, seventeen years later you're sittin' here smack- dab in front of me, hail and hearty as cake. Except for your tongue. Talk, Dickie Bird Halked, talk. Say somethin'. Come on. Try this: "Daddy, daddy, daddy."
Dickie Bird shakes his head.
Come on. Just this once. Maybe it will work.
Takes Dickie Bird by the cheeks with one hand.
"Daddy, daddy, daddy, daddy."
Dickie Bird jumps up and attacks Pierre, looking as though he were about to shove the crucifix down Pierre's throat. Pierre is genuinely terrified. Just then, Spooky re-enters with the skate.
Whoa, whoa. Easy. Easy now, Dickie Bird. Easy.
SPOOKY:
Gasping again at the sight of Dickie Bird man-handling the crucifix, he makes a bee-line for the boy.
Dickie Bird Halked? Give me that thing.
And grabs the crucifix with a flourish. Then he turns to Pierre and holds the skate out with his other hand.
Promise.
PIERRE:
Cross my heart.
Crosses himself.
SPOOKY:
Replacing the crucifix on the wall and pointing at Pierre.
The Lord.

PIERRE:
The Lord.
Spooky hands the skate over to Pierre. Just then, Creature Nataways stumbles in, now visibly drunk.

CREATURE:
The Lord!
Picking on the hapless Dickie Bird, Creature roughly shoves the boy down to a chair.

PIERRE:
Holding up both his skates.
I got 'em both. See? I got 'em.

CREATURE:
Hallelujah! Now all you gotta do is learn how to skate.

SPOOKY:
Creature Nataways, I don't want you in my house in that condition. Lalala is liable to pop any minute now and I don't want my son to see the first thing he sees when he comes into the world is a drunk..

PIERRE:
Damn rights!

SPOOKY:
...you too, Pierre St. Pierre.

CREATURE:
Aw! William Lacroix, don't give me that holier than-me, poker-up-the-bum spiritual bull crap....

SPOOKY:
...say wha?...

CREATURE:
Are you preachin' to this boy, William Lacroix? Are you usin' him again to practice your preachy-preachy? Don't do that, William, the boy is helpless. If you wanna practice, go practice on your old buddy, go preach on Big Joey. He's the one who needs it.

SPOOKY:
You're hurting again, aren't you, Creature Nataways.

CREATURE:
Don't listen to Spooky Lacroix, Dickie Bird. You follow Spooky Lacroix and you go right down to the dogs, I'm tellin' you that right now. Hair spray, lysol, vanilla extract, shoe polish, xerox machine juice, he's done it all, this man. If you'd given William Lacroix the chance, he'd have sliced up the Xerox machine and ate it...

PIERRE:
Mockingly, in the background.
No!

CREATURE:
...He once drank a Kitty Wells record. He lied to his own mother and he stole her record and he boiled it and swallowed it right up...

PIERRE:
Good heavens!
Big Joey enters and stands at the door unseen.

CREATURE:
...Made the Globe and Mail, too. He's robbed, he's cheated his best friend...

SPOOKY:
Alphonse Nataways? Why are you doing this, may I ask?

CREATURE:
Oh, he was bad, Dickie Bird Halked, he was bad. Fifteen years. Fifteen years of his life pukin' his guts out on sidewalks from here to Sicamous, B.C., this man...

SPOOKY:
Shush!

CREATURE:
...and this is the same man...

BIG JOEY:
Speaking suddenly and laughing, he takes everyone by suprise. They gasp. And practically freeze in their tracks.
...who's yellin' and preachin' about "the Lord!" They oughta retire the beaver and put this guy on the Canadian nickel, he's become a national goddamn symbol, that what you're sayin', Creature Nataways? This the kind of man you wanna become, that what you're sayin' to the boy, Creature Nataways?
Close up to Dickie Bird.
A man who couldn't get a hard-on in front of a woman if you paid him a two dollar bill!

SPOOKY:
Stung to the quick.
And is this the kind of man you wanna become, Dickie Bird Halked, this MAN who can't take the sight of blood least of all woman's blood, this MAN who, when he sees a woman's blood, chokes up, pukes and faints, how do you like that?
Pierre, sensing potential violence, begins to sneak out.

BIG JOEY:
Pulls a bottle out of his coat.
Spooky Lacroix, igwani eeweepoonaskeewuk. ("The end of the world is at hand.")
Pierre, seeing the bottle, retraces his steps and sits down again, grabbing a tea-cup en route, ready for a drink.

SPOOKY:
Shocked.
Get that thing out of my house!

BIG JOEY:

Tonight, we're gonna celebrate my wife, Spooky Lacroix, we're gonna celebrate because my wife, the fabulous, the incredible Gazelle Delphina Nataways has been crowned Captain of the Wasy Wailerettes. The Rez is makin' history, Spooky Lacroix. The world will never be the same. Come on, it's on me, it's on your old buddy, the old, old buddy you said you'd never, ever forget.

SPOOKY:

I told you a long time ago, Big Joey, after what you went and done to my sister, this here boy's own mother, you're no buddy of mine. Get out of my house. Get!

BIG JOEY:

Handing the bottle of whiskey to Creature.
Creature Nataways, celebrate your wife.

CREATURE:

Raising the bottle in a toast.
To my wife!

PIERRE:

Holding his cup out to the bottle.
Your ex-wife.

BIG JOEY:

Suddenly quiet and intimate.
William. William. You and me. You and me, we used to be buddies, kigiskisin? ("Remember?") Wounded Knee. South Dakota. Spring of '73. We parked my van over by that little lake, we swam across, you almost didn't make it and nothin' could get you to swim back. Kigiskisin? So here we're walkin' back through the bush, all the way around this small lake, nothin' on but bare feet and wet undershorts and this black bear come up behind you, kigiskisin? And you freaked out. *Laughs. Pierre tries, as best he can, to create a party*

atmosphere, to little avail. Creature nervously watches
Big Joey and Spooky. Dickie Bird merely sits there,
head down, rocking back and forth.

SPOOKY:
Obviously extremely uncomfortable.
You freaked out too, ha-ha, ha-ha.

BIG JOEY:
That bear gave you a real spook, huh?
Pause. Then, suddenly, he jumps at the other men.
Boo!
The other men, including Spooky, jump, splashing
whiskey all over the place. Big Joey laughs. The other
men pretend to laugh.
That's how you got your name, you old Spook...

SPOOKY:
You were scared too, ha-ha, ha-ha.

BIG JOEY:
...we get back to the camp and there's Creature and
Eugene and Zach and Roscoe, bacon and eggs all ready
for us. Christ, I never laughed so hard in my life. But
here you were, not laughin' and we'd say: "What's the
matter, Spook, you don't like our jokes? And you'd say:
"That's good, yeah, that's good." I guess you were
laughin' from a different part of yourself, huh? You
were beautiful...

SPOOKY:
That's good, yeah, that's good.

BIG JOEY:
Getting the bottle back from Creature and Pierre.
So tonight, Bear-who-went-and-gave-you-a-real-Spooky
Lacroix, we're gonna celebrate another new page in our
lives. Wounded Knee Three! Women's version!

PIERRE:
Damn rights.

BIG JOEY:

Raising the bottle up in a toast.

To my wife!

SPOOKY:

Ha! Get that thing away from me.

PIERRE:

Spooky Lacroix, co-operate. Co-operate for once. The women, the women are playin' hockey.

CREATURE:

To my wife!

PIERRE:

Your ex-wife.

CREATURE:

Shut up you toothless old bugger.

SPOOKY:

Big Joey, you're not my friend no more.

BIG JOEY:

Finally grabbing Spooky roughly by the throat. Creature jumps to help hold Spooky still.

You never let a friend for life go, William Hector Lacroix, not even if you turn your back on your own father, Nicotine Lacroix's spiritual teachings and pretend like hell to be this born-again Christian.

SPOOKY:

Let go, Creature Nataways, let go of me!

To Big Joey.

For what you did to this boy at that bar seventeen years ago, Joseph Jeremiah McLeod, you are going to hell. To hell!

Big Joey baptizes Spooky with the remainder of the bottle's contents. Breaking free, Spooky grabs Dickie Bird and shoves him toward Big Joey.

Look at him. He can't even talk. He hasn't talked in seventeen years!

Dickie Bird cries out, breaks free, grabs the crucifix from off the wall and runs out the door, crying. Spooky breaks down, falls to the floor and weeps. Big Joey attempts to pick him up gently, but Spooky kicks him away.

Let go of me! Let go!

CREATURE:

Lifting the empty bottle, laughing and crying at the same time.

To my wife, to my wife, to my wife, to my wife, to my wife...

Big Joey suddenly lifts Spooky off the floor by the collar and lifts a fist to punch his face. Black-out.

Out of this black-out emerges the eery, distant sound of women wailing and pucks hitting boards, echoing and echoing as in a vast empty chamber. The lights come up on Dickie Bird Halked and Simon Starblanket, standing beside each other in the "bleachers" of the hockey arena, watching the "ice" area (i.e., looking out over the audience). The "bleachers" area is actually on the upper level of the set, in a straight line directly in front of Nanabush's perch. Dickie Bird is still holding Spooky's crucifix and Simon is still holding his dancing bustle.

SIMON:

Your grandpa, Nicotine Lacroix, was a medicine man. Hell of a name, but he was a medicine man. Old priest here, Father Boucher, years ago — oh, he was a terrible man — he went and convinced the people old Nicotine Lacroix talked to the devil. That's not true. Nicotine Lacroix was a good man. That's why I want you for my best man. Me and Patsy are getting married a couple of months from now. It's decided. We're gonna have a baby. Then we're going down to South Dakota and we're gonna dance with the Rosebud Sioux this summer.

Sings as he stomps his foot in the rhythm of a pow-wow drum.

"...and me I don't wanna go to the moon, I'm gonna leave that moon alone. I just wanna dance with the Rosebud Sioux this summer, yeah, yeah, yeah..."

And he breaks into a chant. Dickie Bird watches, fascinated, particularly by the bustle Simon holds up in the air.

At this point, Zachary Jeremiah Keechigeesik approaches timidly from behind a beam, his pants held flimsily together with a huge safety pin. The sound of women wailing and pucks hitting boards now shifts into the sound of an actual hockey arena, just before a big game.

ZACHARY:

To Simon.

Hey!

But Simon doesn't hear and continues chanting.

Pssst!

SIMON:

Zachary Jeremiah. Neee, watstagatch!

ZACHARY:

Is Hera out there?

SIMON:

Indicating the "ice."

Yup. There she is.

ZACHARY:

Lordy, lordy, lordy...

SIMON:

Just kidding. She's not out there...

ZACHARY:
Don't do that to me!

SIMON:
...yet.

ZACHARY:
Finally coming up to join the young men at the "bleachers."
You know that Nanabush character you were telling me about a couple of nights ago? What do you say I give his name over to them little gingerbread cookie men I'm gonna be making? For starters. Think that would help any?

SIMON:
Neee...
Just then, Big Joey enters and proceeds to get a microphone stand ready for broadcasting the game. Zachary recoils and goes to stand as far away from him as possible.

ZACHARY:
Looking out over the "ice."
It's almost noon. They're late getting started.

BIG JOEY:
Yawning luxuriously.
That's right. Me and Gazelle Nataways...slept in.
Creature Nataways comes scurrying in.

CREATURE:
Still talking to himself.
...I tole you once I tole you twice...
Then to the other men.
Chris' sakes! Are they really gonna do it? Chris' sakes!
Spooky Lacroix enters wearing a woolen scarf he obviously knitted himself. He is still knitting, this time a pale blue baby sweater. He also now sports a black eye and band-aide on his face. All the men, except Pierre St. Pierre, are now in the "bleachers," standing

in a straight line facing the audience, with Dickie Bird in the center area, Simon and Spooky to his immediate right and left, respectively.

SPOOKY:

It's bad luck to start late. I know. I read the interview with Gay Lafleur in last week's Expositor. They won't get far.

He sees Gazelle Nataways entering the "rink," unseen by the audience. (All the hockey players on the "ice" are unseen by the audience; it is only the men who can actually "see" them.)

Look! Gazelle Nataways went and got her sweater trimmed in the chest area!

Wild cat calls from the men.

CREATURE:

Trimmed it? She's got it plunging down to her ootsee. ("belly button.")

ZACHARY:

Ahem. Smokes too much. Lung problems.

BIG JOEY:

Nah. More like it's got somethin' to do with the undershorts she's wearin' today.

ZACHARY:

Fast on the up-take.

Fuck you!

BIG JOEY:

Blowing Zachary a kiss.

Poosees. ("Pussy cat." [Zachary's childhood nick name.])

SPOOKY:

Terrible. Terrible. Tsk, tsk, tsk.

Pierre St. Pierre enters on the lower level, teetering dangerously on his skates towards the "ice" area down-stage. He wears a referee's top and a whistle around his neck.

PIERRE:

Checking the names off as he reads from a clipboard.
Dominique Ladouche, Black Lady Halked, Annie Cook,
June Bug McLeod, Big Bum Pegahmagahbow . . .

SIMON:

Calling out.
Patsy Pegahmagahbow, turkey.

PIERRE:

Shut up. I'm workin' here. ...Leonarda Lee Star-
blanket, that terrible Dictionary woman, Fluffy Sainte-
Marie, Chicken Lips Pegahmagahbow, Dry Lips
Manigitogan, Little Hand Manigitogan, Little Girl
Manitowabi, Victoria Manitowabi, Belinda Nickikoo-
simeenicaning, Martha Two-Axe Early-in-the-Morn-
ing, her royal highness Gazelle Delphina Nataways,
Delia Opekokew, Barbra Nahwegahbow, Gloria May
Eshkibok, Hera Keechigeesik, Tall Mary Ann Patch-
nose, Short Mary Ann Patchnose, Queen Elizabeth
Patchnose, the triplets Marjorie Moose, Maggie May
Moose, Mighty Moose and, of course, my wife, Veronique
St. Pierre. Yup. They're all there, I hope, and the world
is about to explode!

SPOOKY:

That's what I've been trying to tell you!
*Pierre St. Pierre, barely able to stand on his skates,
hobbles about, obviously getting almost trampled by
the hockey players at various times.*

BIG JOEY:

*Now speaking on the microphone. The other men
watch the women on the "ice"; some are cheering and
whistling, some calling down the game.*
Welcome, ladies igwa gentlemen, welcome one and all
to the Wasaychigan Hill Hip-hip-hippodrome. This is
your host for the big game, Big Joey — and they don't

call me Big Joey for nothin' — Chairman, CEO and Proprietor of the Wasaychigan Hill Hippodrome, bringin' you a game such as has never been seen ever before on the ice of any hockey arena anywhere on the island of Manitoulin, anywhere on the face of this country, anywhere on the face of this planet. And there...

CREATURE:
...there's Gazelle Nataways, number one...

BIG JOEY:
...they are, ladies...

SPOOKY:
...terrible, terrible...

BIG JOEY:
...igwa gentlemen...

CREATURE:
...Chris'sakes, that's my wife, Chris'sakes...

BIG JOEY:
...there they are, the most beautiful...

SIMON:
...give 'em hell, Patsy Pegahmagahbow, give 'em hell...

BIG JOEY:
...daring, death-...

SIMON:
To Zachary.
...there's Hera Keechigeesik, number nine...

BIG JOEY:
...defying Indian women...

SPOOKY:
...terrible, terrible...

BIG JOEY:
...in the world...

ZACHARY:
...that's my wife...

BIG JOEY:
...the Wasy Wailerettes...

Clears his throat and tests the microphone by tapping it gently.

ZACHARY:

...lordy, lordy, lordy...

CREATURE:

Hey, Gazelle Nataways and Hera Keechigeesik are lookin' at each other awful funny. Something bad's gonna happen, I tole you once I tole you twice, something bad's gonna happen...

SPOOKY:

This is sign from the Lord. This is THE sign...

BIG JOEY:

Number One Gazelle Nataways, Captain of the Wasy Wailerettes, facing off with Number Nine, Flora McDonald, Captain of the Canoe Lake Bravettes. And referee Pierre St. Pierre drops the puck and takes off like a herd of wild turtles...

SIMON:

Aw, Spooky Lacroix, eat my shitty shorts, neee...

BIG JOEY:*

...Hey, aspin Number Six Dry Lips Manigitogan, rightwinger for the Wasy Wailerettes...

ZACHARY:

...look pretty damn stupid, if you ask me. Fifteen thousand dollars for all that new equipment...

BIG JOEY:

...eemaskamat Number Thirteen of the Canoe Lake Bravettes anee-i puck...

CREATURE:

...Cancel the game! Cancel the game! Cancel the game! ...

Etc.

---

* the following hockey commentary by Big Joey (pages 71-74) is translated on pages 131-132.

BIG JOEY:

...igwa aspin sipweesinskwataygew. Hey, k'seegoochin!
Off Microphone.
Creature Nataways. Shut up.
To the other men.
Get this asshole out of here....

SIMON:

Yay, Patsy Pegahmagahbow! Pat-see! Pat-see! Pat-see!...
Etc.

BIG JOEY:

Back on microphone.
...How, Number Six Dry Lips Manigitogan, right-winger for the Wasy Wailerettes, soogi pugamawew igwa anee-i puck igwa aspin center-line ispathoo ana puck...

CREATURE:

To Simon.
Shut up. Don't encourage them...

BIG JOEY:

...ita Number Nine Hera Keechigeesik, left-winger for...

SIMON:

To Creature.
Aw, lay off! Pat-see! Pat-see! Pat-see!...
Etc.

BIG JOEY:

...the Wasy Wailerettes, kagatchitnat. How, Number Nine Hera Keechigeesik...
He continues uninterrupted.

CREATURE:

...Stop the game! Stop the game! Stop the game!...
Etc.

ZACHARY:

Goodness sakes, there's gonna be fight out there!

Creature continues his "stop the game," Zachary repeats "goodness sakes, there's gonna be a fight out there," Simon's "Pat-see!" has now built up into a full chant, his foot pounding on the floor so that it sounds like a powwow drum, his dancing bustle held aloft like a shield. Spooky finally grabs the crucifix away from Dickie Bird, holds it aloft and begins to pray, loudly, as in a ceremony. Dickie Bird, caught between Simon's chanting and Spooky's praying, blocks his ears with his hands and looks with growing consternation at "the game." Pierre blows his whistle and skates around like a puppet gone mad.

SPOOKY:
The Lord is my shepherd; I shall not want. He maketh me to lie down in green pastures; he leadeth me beside the still waters. He restoreth my soul; he leadeth me in the paths of righteousness for his name's sake. Yea, though I walk through the valley of the shadow of death, I will fear no evil; for thou art with me. Yea, though I walk through the valley of the shadow of death, I will fear no evil; for thou art with me...

He repeats this last phrase over and over again. Finally, Dickie Bird freaks out, screams and runs down to the "ice" area.

BIG JOEY:
Continuing uninterrupted above all the other men's voices.
...igwa ati-ooteetum blue line ita Number One Gazelle Nataways, Captain of the Wasy Wailerettes, kagag-weemaskamat anee-i puck, ma-a Number Nine Hera Keechigeesik mawch weemeethew anee-i puck. Wha! "Hooking," itwew referee Pierre St. Pierre, Gazelle Nataways isa keehookiwatew her own team-mate Hera Keechigeesikwa, wha! How, Number One Gazelle Nataways, Captain of the Wasy Wailerettes, face-

off igwa meena itootum asichi Number Nine Flora McDonald, Captain of the Canoe Lake Bravettes igwa Flora McDonald soogi pugamawew anee-i puck, ma-a Number Thirty-seven Big Bum Pegahmagahbow, defense-woman for the Wasy Wailerettes, stops the puck and passes it to Number Eleven Black Lady Halked, also defense-woman for the Wasy Wailerettes, but Gazelle Nataways, Captain of the Wasy Wailerettes, soogi body check meethew her own team-mate Black Lady Halked woops! She falls, ladies igwa qentlemen, Black Lady Halked hits the boards and Black Lady Halked is singin' the blues, ladies igwa gentlemen, Black Lady Halked sings the blues.

Off microphone, to the other men.

What the hell is goin' on down there? Dickie Bird, get off the ice!

Back on microphone.

Wha! Number Eleven Black Lady Halked is up in a flash igwa seemak n'taymaskamew Gazelle Nataways anee-i puck, holy shit! The ailing but very, very furious Black Lady Halked skates back, turns and takes aim, it's gonna be a slap shot, ladies igwa gentlemen, slap shot keetnatch taytootum Black Lady Halked igwa Black Lady Halked shootiwoo anee-i puck, wha! She shoots straight at her very own captain, Gazelle Nataways and holy shit, holy shit, holy fuckin' shit!

All hell breaks loose; it is as though some bizarre dream has entered the arena. We hear the sound of women wailing and pucks hitting boards, echoing and echoing as in a vast empty chamber. The men are all screaming at the same time, from the "bleachers," re-calling Black Lady Halked's legendary fall of seventeen years ago.

BIG JOEY:

Dropping his microphone in horror.
Holy Christ! If there is a devil in this world, then he has just walked into this room. Holy Christ!...
He says this over and over again.

ZACHARY:

Do something about her, goodness sakes, I told you guys to do something about her seventeen years ago, but you wouldn't do fuck-all. So go out there now and help her...
Repeated.

CREATURE:

Never mind, Chris'sakes, don't bother her. Let me out of here. Chris'sakes, let me out of here!...
Repeated.

SPOOKY:

...Yea, though I walk through the valley of the shadow of death, I will fear no evil; for thou art with me...
Repeated. While Simon continues chanting and stomping.

PIERRE:

From the "ice" area.
Never you mind, Zachary Jeremiah, never you mind. She'll be okay. No she won't. Zachary Jeremiah, go out there and help her. No. She'll be okay. No she won't. Yes. No. Yes. No. Help! Where's the puck? Can't do nothin' without the goddamn puck. Where's the puck?! Where's the puck?! Where's the puck?!...
He repeats this last phrase over and over again. Center- and down-stage, on the "ice" area, Dickie Bird is going into a complete "freak-out," breaking into a grotesque, fractured version of a Cree chant.

Gradually, Big Joey, Zachary and Creature join Pierre's refrain of "where's the puck?!", with which they all, including the chanting Simon and the praying Spooky, scatter and come running down to the "ice" area. As they reach the lower level and begin to approach the audience, their movements break down into slow motion, as though they were trying to run through the sticky, gummy substance of some horrible, surrealistic nightmare.

PIERRE/BIG JOEY/ZACHARY/CREATURE:

Slower and slower, as on a record that is slowing down gradually to a stop.

Where's the puck?! Where's the puck?! Where's the puck?!...

Etc..

Simon continues chanting and stomping, Spooky continues intoning the last phrase of his prayer and Dickie Bird continues his fractured chant. Out of this fading "sound collage" emerges the sound of a jukebox playing the introduction to Kitty Wells' "It Wasn't God Who Made Honky Tonk Angels," as though filtered through memory. At this point, on the upper level, a giant luminescent hockey stick comes seemingly out of nowhere and, in very slow motion, shoots a giant luminescent puck. On the puck, looking like a radiant but damaged "Madonna-with-child," sits Nanabush, as the spirit of Black Lady Halked, naked, nine months pregnant, drunk almost senseless and barely able to hold a bottle of beer up to her mouth. All the men freeze in their standing positions facing the audience, except for Dickie Bird who continues his fractured chanting and whimpering, holding his arms up towards Nanabush/Black Lady Halked. The giant luminescent puck reaches and stops at the edge

of the upper level. Nanabush/Black Lady Halked
struggles to stand and begins staggering toward her
perch. She reaches it and falls with one arm on top of
it. The magical, glittering lights flare on and, for the
first time, the jukebox is revealed. Nanabush/Black
Lady Halked staggers laboriously up to the top of the
jukebox and stands there in profile, one arm lifted to
raise her beer as she pours it over her belly. Behind
her, the full moon begins to glow, blood red. And
from the jukebox, Kitty Wells sings:

As I sit here tonight, the jukebox playing,
That tune about the wild side of life;
As I listen to the words you are saying,
It brings memories when I was a trusting wife.

It wasn't God who made honky tonk angels,
As you said in the words of your song;
Too many times married men think they're still single,
That has caused many a good girl to go wrong.

During the "instrumental break" of the song here,
Dickie Bird finally explodes and shrieks out towards
the vision of Nanabush/Black Lady Halked.
DICKIE BIRD:
Mama! Mama! Katha paksini. Katha paksini. Kana-
wapata wastew. Kanawapataw wastew. Michimina.
Michimina. Katha pagitina. Kaweechee-ik nipapa.
Kaweechee-ik nipapa. Nipapa. Papa. Papa. Papa.
Papa. Papa. Papa! ("Mommy! Mommy! Don't fall.
Don't fall. Look at the light. Look at the light. Hold
on to it. Hold on to it. Don't let it go. My daddy will
help you. My daddy will help you. My daddy. Daddy.
Daddy. ETC.")

He crumples to the floor and freezes. Kitty Wells sings:

It's a shame that all the blame is on us women,
It's not true that only you men feel the same;
From the start most every heart that's ever broken,
Was because there always was a man to blame.

It wasn't God who made honky tonk angels;
As you said in the words of your song;
Too many times married men think they're still single,
That has caused many a good girl to go wrong.

As the song fades, the final tableau is one of Dickie Bird collapsed on the floor between Simon, who is holding aloft his bustle, and Spooky, who is holding aloft his crucifix, directly in front of and at the feet of Big Joey and, above Big Joey, the pregnant Nanabush/ Black Lady Halked, who is standing on top of the flashing jukebox, in silhouette against the full moon, bottle held up above her mouth. Zachary, Creature and Pierre are likewise frozen, standing off to the side of this central grouping. Slow fade-out.

End of Act One.

Act Two

When the lights come up, Dickie Bird Halked is standing on a rock in the forest, his clothes and hair all askew. He holds Spooky's crucifix, raised with one hand up to the night sky; he is trying, as best he can, to chant, after Simon Starblanket's fashion. As he does, Nanabush appears in the shadows a distance behind him (as the spirit of Gazelle Nataways, minus the gigantic breasts, but dressed, this time, as a stripper). She lingers and watches with interest. Slowly, Dickie Bird climbs off the rock and walks off-stage, his quavering voice fading into the distance. The full moon glows. Fade-out.

Fade-in on Spooky Lacroix's kitchen, where Spooky is busy pinning four little pale blue baby booties on the wall where the crucifix used to be, the booties that, in Act One, covered the four extremities of the crucifix. At the table are Pierre St. Pierre and Zachary Jeremiah Keechigeesik. Pierre is stringing pale blue yarn around Zachary's raised, parted hands. Then Spooky joins them at the table and begins knitting again, this time, a baby bonnet, also pale blue. Zachary sits removed through most of this scene, pre-occupied with the problem of his still missing shorts, his bakery and his wife. The atmosphere is one of fear and foreboding, almost as though the men were constantly resisting the impulse to look over their shoulders. On the upper level, in a soft, dim light, Nanabush/Gazelle can be seen sitting up on her perch, waiting impatiently for "the boys" to finish their talk.

PIERRE:

In a quavering voice.

The Wasy Wailerettes are dead. Gentlemen, my job is disappeared from underneath my feet.

SPOOKY:

And we have only the Lord to thank for that.

PIERRE:

Gazelle Nataways, she just sashayed herself off that ice, behind swayin' like a walrus pudding. That game, gentlemen, was what I call a real apostrophe...

ZACHARY:

Catastrophe.

PIERRE:

That's what I said, dammit....

SPOOKY:

...tsk...

PIERRE:

...didn't even get to referee more than ten minutes. But you have to admit, gentlemen, that slap shot...

SPOOKY:

...that's my sister, Black Lady Halked, that's my sister...

PIERRE:

...did you see her slap shot? Fantastic! Like a bullet, like a killer shark. Unbelievable!

ZACHARY:

Uncomfortable.

Yeah, right.

PIERRE:
When Black Lady Halked hit Gazelle Nataways with that puck. Them Nataways eyes. Big as plates!

SPOOKY:
Bigger than a ditch!

PIERRE:
Them mascara stretch marks alone was a perfectly frightful thing to behold. Holy shit la marde! But you know, they couldn't find that puck.

SPOOKY:
Losing his cool and laughing, falsely and nervously.
Did you see it? It fell...it fell...that puck went splat on her chest...and it went...it went...plummety plop...

PIERRE:
...plummety plop to be sure...

SPOOKY:
...down her...down her...

PIERRE:
Down the crack. Right down that horrendous, scarifyin' Nataways bosom crack.
The "kitchen lights" go out momentarily and, to the men, inexplicably. Then they come back on. The men look about them, perplexed.

SPOOKY:
Serves...her...right for trimming her hockey sweater in the chest area, is what I say.

PIERRE:
They say that puck slid somewhere deep, deep into the folds of her fleshy, womanly juices...

ZACHARY:
...there's a lot of things they're saying about that puck...

PIERRE:
...and it's lost. Disappeared. Gone. Phhht! Nobody can find that puck.

At this point, Spooky gets up to check the light switch. The lights go out.

ZACHARY:

In the darkness.

Won't let no one come near her, is what they say. Not six inches.

PIERRE:

I gotta go look for that puck.

Lights come back on. Pierre inexplicably appears sitting in another chair.

Gentlemen, I gotta go jiggle that woman.

Lights out again.

ZACHARY:

From the darkness.

What's the matter, Spook?

SPOOKY:

Obviously quite worried.

Oh, nothing, nothing...

Lights come back on. Pierre appears sitting back in his original chair. The men are even more mystified, but try to brighten up anyway.

...just...checking the lights... Queen of the Indians, that's what she tried to look like, walking off that ice.

PIERRE:

Queen of the Indians, to be sure. That's when them women went and put their foot down and made up their mind, on principle, no holds barred...

A magical flash of lavender light floods the room very briefly, establishing a connection between Spooky's kitchen and Nanabush's perch, where Nanabush/ Gazelle is still sitting, tapping her fingers impatiently, looking over her shoulder periodically, as if to say: "come on, boys, get with it." Pierre's speech momentarily goes into slow motion.

...no...way...they're ...takin' up...them hockey sticks again until that particular puck is found. "The particular puck," that's what they call it. Gentlemen, the Wasy Wailerettes are dead. My job is disappeared. Gone. Kaput kaput. Phhht!

SPOOKY:

Amen.

Pause. Thoughtful silence for a beat or two.

ZACHARY:

W-w-w-where's that nephew of yours, Spook?

SPOOKY:

Dickie Bird Halked?

PIERRE:

My wife, Veronique St. Pierre, she informs me that Dickie Bird Halked, last he was seen, was pacin' the bushes in the general direction of the Pegahmagahbow acreage near Buzwah, lookin' for all the world like he had lost his mind, poor boy.

ZACHARY:

Lordy, lordy, lordy, I'm telling you right now, Spooky Lacroix, if you don't do something about that nephew of yours, he's liable to go out there and kill someone next time.

SPOOKY:

I'd be out there myself pacing the bushes with him except my wife Lalala's liable to pop any minute now and I gotta be ready to zip her up to Sudbury General.

PIERRE:

Bah. Them folks of his, they don't care. If it's not hockey, it's bingo she's out playin' every night of the week, that Black Lady of a mother of his.

ZACHARY:

Went and won the jackpot again last night, Black Lady Halked did. All fifty pounds of it...

PIERRE:

Beat Gazelle Nataways by one number!

ZACHARY:

...if it wasn't for her, I'd have mastered that apple pie recipe by now. I was counting on all that lard. Fifty pounds, goodness sakes.

SPOOKY:

This little old kitchen? It's yours, Zachary Jeremiah, anytime, anytime. Lalala's got tons of lard.

PIERRE:

Ha! She better have. Zachary Jeremiah hasn't dared go nowhere near his own kitchen in almost a week.

ZACHARY:

Four nights! It's only Wednesday night, Pierre St. Pierre. Don't go stretching the truth just cuz you were too damn chicken to go get me my shorts.

PIERRE:

Bah!

SPOOKY:

To Zachary.

Your shorts?

ZACHARY:

Evading the issue.

I just hope that Black Lady Halked's out there looking after her boy cuz if she isn't, we're all in a heap of trouble, I have a funny feeling.

Suddenly, he throws the yarn down and rises.

Achh! I've got to cook!

He goes behind the kitchen counter, puts an apron on and begins the preparations for making pie pastry.

SPOOKY:

To Pierre, half-whispering.

His shorts?

Pierre merely shrugs, indicating Zachary's pants, which are still held together with a large safety pin. Spooky and Pierre laugh nervously. Spooky looks concernedly at the four little booties on the wall where the crucifix used to be. Beat.

Suddenly, Pierre slaps the table with one hand and leans over to Spooky, all set for an argument, an argument they've obviously had many times before. Through all this, Zachary is making pie pastry at the counter and Spooky continues knitting. The atmosphere of "faked" jocular camaraderie grows, particularly as the music gets louder later on. Nanabush/ Gazelle is now getting ready for her strip in earnest, standing on her perch, spraying perfume on, stretching her legs, etc. The little tivoli lights in the jukebox begin to twinkle little by little.

PIERRE:
Queen of Hearts.

SPOOKY:
Belvedere.

PIERRE:
Queen of Hearts.

SPOOKY:
The Belvedere.

PIERRE:
I told you many times, Spooky Lacroix, it was the Queen of Hearts. I was there. You were there. Zachary Jeremiah, Big Joey, Creature Nataways, we were all there.

From here on, the red/blue/purple glow of the jukebox (i.e. Nanabush's perch) becomes more and more apparent.

SPOOKY:

And I'm telling you it was the Belvedere Hotel, before it was even called the Belvedere Hotel, when it was still called...

PIERRE:

Spooky Lacroix, don't contribute your elder. Big Joey, may he rot in hell, he was the bouncer there that night, he was right there the night it happened.

ZACHARY:

Hey, Spook. Where do you keep your rolling pin?

SPOOKY:

Use my salami.

PIERRE:

To Spooky.

He was there.

ZACHARY:

Big Joey was never the bouncer, he was the janitor.

SPOOKY:

At the Belvedere Hotel.

PIERRE:

Never you mind, Spooky Lacroix, never you mind. Black Lady Halked was sittin' there in her corner of the bar for three weeks...

SPOOKY:

Three weeks?! It was more like three nights. Aw, you went and mixed up my baby's cap.

Getting all tangled up with his knitting.

ZACHARY:

Got any cinnamon?

SPOOKY:

I got chili powder. Same color as cinnamon.

Faintly, the strip music from the jukebox begins to play.

PIERRE:

...the place was so jam-packed with people drinkin' beer and singin' and smokin' cigarettes and watchin' the dancin' girl...

SPOOKY:

...Gazelle Nataways, she was the dancing girl...

The music is now on full volume and Nanabush/Gazelle's strip is in full swing. She dances on top of the jukebox, which is now a riot of sound and flashing lights. Spooky's kitchen is bathed in a gorgeous lavender light. Big Joey and Creature Nataways appear at Spooky's table, each drinking a bottle of beer. The strip of seventeen years ago is fully recreated, the memory becoming so heated that Nanabush/Gazelle magically appears dancing right on top of Spooky's kitchen table. The men are going wild, applauding, laughing, drinking, all in slow motion and in mime. In the heat of the moment, as Nanabush/Gazelle strips down to silk tassels and G-string, they begin tearing their clothes off.

Suddenly, Simon Starblanket appears at Spooky's door: Nanabush/Gazelle disappears, as do Big Joey and Creature. And Spooky, Pierre and Zachary are caught with their pants down. The jukebox music fades.

SIMON:

Spooky Lacroix.

The lavender light snaps off, we are back to "reality" and Spooky, Pierre and Zachary stand there, embarrassed. In a panic, they begin putting their clothes back on and reclaim the positions they had before the strip. Spooky motions Simon to take a seat at the table. Simon does so.

Spooky Lacroix. Rosie Kakapetum expresses interest in coming here to birth Lalala's baby when the time comes.

SPOOKY:
Rosie Kakapetum? No way some witch is gonna come and put her witchy little fingers on my baby boy.

SIMON:
Rosie Kakapetum's no witch, Spooky Lacroix. She's Patsy Pegahmagahbow's step-mother and she's Wasy's only surviving medicine woman and mid-wife...

SPOOKY:
Hogwash!

PIERRE:
Ahem. Rosie Kakapetum says it's a cryin' shame the Wasy Wailerettes is the only team that's not in the Ontario Hockey League.

ZACHARY:
Ontario Hockey League?

PIERRE:
Absolutely. The OHL. Indian women's OHL. All the Indian women in Ontario's playin' hockey now. It's like a fever out there.

ZACHARY:
Shoot.
Referring to his pastry.
I hope this new recipe works for me.

PIERRE:
Well, it's not exactly new without the cinnamon.

SPOOKY:
To Simon.
My son will be born at Sudbury General Hospital...

SIMON:
You know what they do to them babies in them city hospitals?

SPOOKY:
...Sudbury General, Simon Starblanket, like any good Christian boy...

PIERRE:
Attempting to diffuse the argument.
Ahem. We got to get them Wasy Wailerettes back on that ice again.

SIMON:
Refusing to let go of Spooky.
They pull them away right from their own mother's breast the minute they come into this world and they put them behind these glass cages together with another two hundred babies like they were some kind of scientific specimens...

PIERRE:
...like two hundred of them little monsters...

ZACHARY:
Hamsters!

PIERRE:
...that's what I said dammit...

SPOOKY:
...tsk...

PIERRE:
...you can't even tell which hamster belongs to which mother. You take Lalala to Sudbury General, Spooky Lacroix, and your hamster's liable to end up stuck to some French lady's tit.

SIMON:
...and they'll hang Lalala up in metal stirrups and your baby's gonna be born going up instead of dropping down which is the natural way. You were born going up instead of dropping down like you should have...

PIERRE:
Yup. You were born at Sudbury General, Spooky

Lacroix, that's why you get weirder and weirder as the days get longer, that's why them white peoples is so weird they were all born going up...

SIMON:

...instead of dropping down...

ZACHARY:

Sprinkling flour in Spooky's face, with both hands, and laughing.

...to the earth, Spooky Lacroix, to the earth...

SPOOKY:

Pooh!

PIERRE:

...but we got to find that puck, Simon Starblanket, them Wasy Wailerettes have got to join the OHL...

SPOOKY:

To Simon.

If Rosie Kakapetum is a medicine woman, Simon Starblanket, then how come she can't drive the madness from my nephew's brain, how come she can't make him talk, huh?

SIMON:

Because the medical establishment and the church establishment and people like you, Spooky Lacroix, have effectively put an end to her usefulness and the usefulness of people like her everywhere, that's why Spooky Lacroix.

SPOOKY:

Phooey!

SIMON:

Do you or your sister even know that your nephew hasn't been home in two days, since that incident at the hockey game, Spooky Lacroix? Do you even care? Why can't you and that thing...

Pointing at the bible that sits beside Spooky.

and all it stands for cure your nephew's madness, as
you call it, Spooky Lacroix? What has this thing...
The bible again.
done to cure the madness of this community and com-
munities like it clean across this country, Spooky Lacroix? Why didn't "the Lord" as you call him, come to
your sister's rescue at that bar seventeen years ago,
huh, Spooky Lacroix?
Pause. Tense silence.
Rosie Kakapetum is gonna be my mother-in-law in
two months, Spooky Lacroix, and if Patsy and I are
gonna do this thing right, if we're gonna work together
to make my best man, Dickie Bird Halked, well again,
then Rosie Kakapetum has got to birth that baby.
He begins to exit.

SPOOKY:
In hard, measured cadence.
Rosie Kakapetum works for the devil.
*Simon freezes in his tracks. Silence. Then he turns,
grabs a chair violently, bangs it down and sits deter-
minedly.*

SIMON:
Fine. I'll sit here and I'll wait.

SPOOKY:
Fine. You sit there and you wait.
*Silence. Simon sits silent and motionless, his back to
the other men.*

PIERRE:
Ahem. Never you mind, Spooky Lacroix, never you
mind. Now as I was sayin', Black Lady Halked was
nine months pregnant when she was sittin' in that
corner of the Queen of Hearts.

SPOOKY:
The Belvedere!

PIERRE:

Three weeks, Black Lady Halked was sittin' there drinkin' beer. They say she got the money by winnin' the jackpot at the Espanola bingo just three blocks down the street. Three weeks, sure as I'm alive and walkin' these treacherous icy roads, three weeks she sat there in that dark corner by herself. They say the only light you could see her by was the light from the jukebox playin' "Rim of Fire" by Johnny Cash...

ZACHARY:

"Rim of Fire." Yeah, right, Pierre St. Pierre.

SPOOKY:

Kitty Wells! Kitty Wells!

The sound of the jukebox playing "It Wasn't God Who Made Honky Tonk Angels" can be heard faintly in the background.

PIERRE:

...the place was so jam-packed with people drinkin' and singin' and smokin' cigarettes and watchin' the dancin' girl...

SPOOKY:

...Gazelle Nataways, she was the dancing girl, Lord save her soul...

PIERRE:

...until Black Lady Halked collapsed...

Spooky, Pierre and Zachary freeze in their positions, looking in horror at the memory of seventeen years ago.

On the upper level, Nanabush, back in her guise as the spirit of Black Lady Halked, sits on the jukebox, facing the audience, legs out directly in front. Nine months pregnant and naked, she holds a bottle of beer up in the air and is drunk almost senseless. The

song, "It Wasn't God Who Made Honky Tonk An-
gels," rises to full volume, the lights from the jukebox
flashing riotously. The full moon glows blood red.
Immediately below Nanabush/Black Lady Halked,
Dickie Bird Halked appears, kneeling, naked, arms
raised toward his mother. Nanabush/Black Lady
Halked begins to writhe and scream, laughing and
crying hysterically at the same time and, as she does,
her water breaks. Dickie Bird, drenched, rises slowly
from the floor, arms still raised, and screams.

DICKIE BIRD:
Mama! Mama!
And from here on, the lights and the sound on this
scene begin to fade slowly, as the scene on the lower
level resumes.

PIERRE:
...she kind of oozed down right then and there, right
down to the floor of the Queen of Hearts Tavern. And
Big Joey, may he rot in hell, he was the bouncer there
that night, when he saw the blood, he ran away and
puked over on the other side of the bar, the sight of all
that woman's blood just scared the shit right out of
him. And that's when Dickie Bird Halked, as we know
him, came ragin'out from his mother's womb, Spooky
Lacroix, in between beers, right there on the floor,
under a table, by the light of the jukebox, on a Saturday
night, at the Queen of Hearts...

SPOOKY:
They went and named him after the bar, you crusted
old fossil! That bar, which is now called the Belvedere
Hotel, used to be called the Dickie Bird Tavern...

SIMON:
Suddenly jumping out of his chair and practically
lunging at Spooky.

It doesn't matter what the fuck the name of that fucking bar was!

The lights and sound on Nanabush and the jukebox have now faded completely.

The fact of the matter is, it never should have happened, that kind of thing should never be allowed to happen, not to us Indians, not to anyone living and breathing on the face of God's green earth.

Pause. Silence. Then, dead calm.

You guys have given up, haven't you? You and your generation. You gave up a long time ago. Scared shitless to face up to the fact it's finally happening, that women are taking power back into their hands, that it was always them — not you, not men — who had the power, the power to give life, the power to keep it. Now you'd rather turn your back on the whole thing and pretend to laugh, wouldn't you.

Silence.

Well, not me. Not us.

Silence.

This is not the kind of Earth we want to inherit.

He begins to leave, but turns once more.

I'll be back. With Patsy. And Rosie.

He exits. Another embarrassed silence.

SPOOKY:

Unwilling to face up to the full horror of it, he chooses, instead, to do exactly what Simon said: turn his back and pretend to laugh.

That bar, which is now called the Belvedere Hotel, used to be called the Dickie Bird Tavern. That's how Dickie Bird Halked got his name. And that's why he goes haywire every now and again and that's why he doesn't talk. Fetal Alcohol something-something, Pierre St. Pierre...

ZACHARY:

From behind the counter, where he is still busy making pie crust.

Fetal Alcohol Syndrome.

SPOOKY:
...that's the devil that stole the baby's tongue because Dickie Bird Halked was born drunk and very, very mad. At the Dickie Bird Tavern in downtown Espanola seventeen years ago and that's a fact.

PIERRE:
Aw, shit la merde. Fuck you, Spooky Lacroix, I'm gonna go get me my rest.
Throws the yarn in Spooky's face, jumps up and exits. Spooky sits there with a pile of yarn stuck to his face, caught on his glasses.

ZACHARY:
Proudly holding up the pie crust in its plate.
It worked!
Black-out.

On the upper level, in a dim light away from her perch, Nanabush/Black Lady Halked is getting ready to go out for the evening, combing her hair in front of a mirror, putting on her clothes, etc. Dickie Bird is with her, naked, getting ready to go to bed. Spooky's crucifix sits on a night-table to the side. In Dickie Bird's mind, he is at home with his mother.

DICKIE BIRD:
Mama. Mama. N'tagoosin. ("I'm sick.")

NANABUSH/BLACK LADY:
Say your prayers.

DICKIE BIRD:
Achimoostawin nimoosoom. ("Tell me about my grandpa.")

NANABUSH/BLACK LADY:
Go to bed. I'm going out soon.

DICKIE BIRD:
Mawch. Achimoostawin nimoosoom. ("No. Tell me about my grandpa.")

NANABUSH/BLACK LADY:
You shouldn't talk about him.

DICKIE BIRD:
Tapweechee eegeemachipoowamit nimoosoom? ("Is it true my grandpa had bad medicine?")

NANABUSH/BLACK LADY :
They say he met the devil once. Your grandpa talked to the devil. Don't talk about him.

DICKIE BIRD:
Eegeemithoopoowamit nimoosoom, eetweet Simon Starblanket. ("Simon Starblanket says he had good medicine.")

NANABUSH/BLACK LADY:
Ashhh! Simon Starblanket.

DICKIE BIRD:
Mawch eemithoosit awa aymeewatik keetnanow kichi, eetweet Simon Starblanket. ("Simon Starblanket says that this cross is not right for us.")
He grabs the crucifix from the night-table and spits on it.

NANABUSH/BLACK LADY:
Grabbing the crucifix from Dickie Bird, she attempts to spank him but Dickie Bird evades her.
Dickie Bird! Kipasta-oon! ("You're committing a mortal sin!") Say ten Hail Marys and two Our Fathers.

DICKIE BIRD:
Mootha apoochiga taskootch nimama keetha. Mootha apoochiga m'tanawgatch kisagee-in. ("You're not even like my mother. You don't even love me at all.")

NANABUSH/BLACK LADY:
Dickie Bird. Shut up. I'll say them with you. "Hail Mary, full of grace, the Lord is with thee..." Hurry up. I have go go out.

As Nanabush/Black Lady Halked now prepares to leave.

"Hail Mary, full of grace, the Lord is with thee..."

She gives up.

Ashhh! Your father should be home soon.

Exits.

DICKIE BIRD:

Speaking out to the now absent Nanabush/Black Lady.

Mootha nipapa ana. ("He's not my father.")

He grabs his clothes and the crucifix and runs out, down to the lower level and into the forest made of light and shadows.

Tapwee anima ka-itweechik, chee-i? Neetha ooma kimineechagan, chee-i? ("It's true what they say, isn't it? I'm a bastard, aren't I?)

He is now sitting on the rock, where Simon and Zachary first met in Act One.

Nipapa ana...Big Joey...

To himself, quietly.

...nipapa ana...Big Joey... ("My father is...Big Joey.")

Silence.

A few moments later, Nanabush comes bouncing into the forest, as the spirit of the vivacious, young Patsy Pegahmagahbow, complete with very large, over-sized bum. The full moon glows.

NANABUSH/PATSY:

To herself, as she peers into the shadows.

Oooh, my poor bum. I fell on the ice four days ago, eh? And it still hurts, oooh.

She finally sees Dickie Bird huddling on the rock, barely dressed.

There you are. I came out to look for you. What happened to your clothes? It's freezing out here. Put them on. Here.

She starts to help dress him.

What happened at the arena? You were on the ice, eh? You feel like talking? In Indian? How, weetamawin. ("Come on, tell me.")

Big Joey and Creature Nataways enter a distance away. They are smoking a joint and Big Joey carries a gun. They stop and watch from the shadows.

CREATURE:

Check her out.

NANABUSH/PATSY:

Why do you always carry that crucifix? I don't believe that stuff. I traded mine in for sweetgrass. Hey. You wanna come to Rosie's and eat fry bread with me? Simon will be there, too. Simon and me, we're getting married, eh? We're gonna have a baby....

CREATURE:

What's she trying to do?

NANABUSH/PATSY:

...Rosie's got deer meat, too, come on, you like my Mom's cooking, eh?

She attempts to take the crucifix away from Dickie Bird.

But you'll have to leave that here because Rosie can't stand the Pope...

Dickie Bird grabs the crucifix back.

CREATURE:

What's he trying to do?

NANABUSH/PATSY:

...give it to me...Dickie...come on...

CREATURE:

He's weird, Big Joey, he's weird.

NANABUSH/PATSY:

...leave it here...it will be safe here...we'll bury it in the snow...

Playfully, she tries to get the crucifix away from Dickie Bird.

CREATURE:

Hey, don't do that, don't do that, man, he's ticklish.

NANABUSH/PATSY:

As Dickie Bird begins poking her playfully with the crucifix and laughing, Nanabush/Patsy gradually starts to get frightened.

...don't look at me that way ...Dickie Bird, what's wrong?...ya, Dickie Bird, awus...

Dickie Bird starts to grab at Nanabush/Patsy.

CREATURE:

Hey, don't you think, don't you think...he's getting kind of carried away?

NANABUSH/PATSY:

...awus...

CREATURE:

We gotta do something, Big Joey, we gotta do something.

Big Joey stops Creature.

Let go! Let go!

NANABUSH/PATSY:

Now in a panic.

...Awus! Awus! Awus!...

Dickie Bird grabs Nanabush/Patsy and throws her violently to the ground, he lifts her skirt and shoves the crucifix up against her.

BIG JOEY:

To Creature.

Shut up.

NANABUSH/PATSY:

Screams and goes into hysteria.

...Simon!...

Dickie Bird rapes Nanabush/Patsy with the crucifix. A heart-breaking, very slow, sensuous tango breaks out on off-stage harmonica.

CREATURE:

To Big Joey.

No! Let me go. Big Joey, let me go, please!

Big Joey suddenly grabs Creature violently by the collar.

BIG JOEY:

Get out. Get the fuck out of here. You're nothin' but a fuckin' fruit. Fuck off.

Creature collapses.

I said fuck off.

Creature flees. Big Joey just stands there, paralyzed, and watches.

Nanabush/Patsy, who has gradually been moving back and back, is now standing up on her perch again (i.e., the "mound"/jukebox which no longer looks like a jukebox). She stands there, facing the audience, and slowly gathers her skirt, in agony, until she is holding it up above her waist. A blood stain slowly spreads across her panties and flows down her leg. At the same time, Dickie Bird stands down-stage beside the rock, holding the crucifix and making violent jabbing motions with it, downward. All this happens in slow motion. The crucifix starts to bleed. When Dickie Bird lifts the crucifix up, his arms and chest are covered with blood. Finally, Nanabush/Patsy collapses to the floor of her platform and slowly crawls away. Lights fade on her. On the lower level, Big Joey, in a state of shock, staggers, almost faints and vomits violently. Then he reels over to Dickie Bird and, not knowing what else to do, begins collecting his clothes and calming him down.

BIG JOEY:

How, Dickie Bird. How, astum. Igwa. Mootha nantow. Mootha nantow. Shhh. Shhh. ("Come on, Dickie Bird. Come. Let's go. It's okay. It's okay. Shhh. Shhh...")

Barely able to bring himself to touch it, he takes the crucifix from Dickie Bird and drops it quickly on the rock. Then he begins wiping the blood off Dickie Bird.

How, mootha nantow. Mootha nantow. How, astum, keeyapitch upisees ootee. Igwani. Igwani. Poonimatoo. Mootha nantow. Mootha nantow. ("Come on, it's okay. It's okay. Come on, a little more over here. That's all. That's all. Stop crying. It's okay. It's okay...")

Dickie Bird, shaking with emotion, looks questioningly into Big Joey's face.

Eehee. Nigoosis keetha. Mootha Wellington Halked kipapa. Neetha...kipapa. ("Yes. You are my son. Wellington Halked is not your father. I'm...your father.")

Silence. They look at each other. Dickie Bird grabs Big Joey and clings to him, Big Joey reacting tentatively, at first, and then passionately, with Dickie Bird finally bursting out into uncontrollable sobs. Fade-out.

Out of this darkness, gunshots explode. And we hear a man's voice wailing, in complete and utter agony. Then comes violent pounding at a door. Finally, still in the darkness, we hear Simon Starblanket's speaking voice.

SIMON:

Open up! Pierre St. Pierre, open up! I know you're in there!

PIERRE:

Still in the darkness.

Whoa! Easy now. Easy on that goddamn door. Must you create such a carpostrophe smack dab in the middle of my rest period?

When the lights come up, we are outside the "window" to Pierre St. Pierre's little boot-leg joint. Pierre pokes his head out, wearing his night clothes, complete with pointy cap.

Go home. Go to bed. Don't be disturbin' my rest period. My wife, Veronique St. Pierre, she tells me there's now not only a OHL but a NHL, too. Indian women's National Hockey League. All the Indian women on every reserve in Canada, all the Indian women in Canada is playin' hockey now. It's like a fever out there. That's why I gotta get my rest. First thing tomorrow mornin', I go jiggle that puck out of Gazelle Nataways. Listen to me. I'm your elder.

Simon shoots the gun into the house, just missing Pierre's head.

SIMON:

Dead calm.

One, you give me a bottle. Two, I report your joint to the Manitowaning police. Three, I shoot your fucking head off.

PIERRE:

Alright. Alright.

He pops in for a bottle of whiskey and hands it out to Simon.

Now you go on home with this. Go have yourself a
nice quiet drink.
Simon begins to exit. Pierre calls out.
What the hell are you gonna do with that gun?
SIMON:
Calling back.
I'm gonna go get that mute. Little bastard raped Patsy
Pegahmagahbow.
Exits.
Pause.
PIERRE:
Holy shit la marde!
Pause.
I gotta warn him. No. I need my rest. No. I gotta warn
that boy. No. I gotta find that puck. No. Dickie Bird's
life. No. The puck. No. Dickie Bird. No. Hockey.
No. His life. No. Hockey. No. Life. Hockey. Life.
Hockey. Life. Hockey. Life. Hockey. Life...
Fade-out.

*Lights up on Spooky Lacroix's kitchen. Creature Na-
taways is sitting at the table, silent, head propped up
in his hands. Spooky is knitting, with obvious haste,
a white christening gown, of which a large crucifix is
the center-piece. Spooky's bible still sits on the table
beside him.*
SPOOKY:
Why didn't you do something?
Silence.
Creature.
Silence. Finally, Spooky stops knitting and looks up.
Alphonse Nataways, why didn't you stop him?
Silence.

You're scared of him, aren't you? You're scared to death of Big Joey. Admit it.

Silence.

CREATURE:

Quietly and calmly.

I love him, Spooky.

SPOOKY:

Say wha?!

CREATURE:

I love him.

SPOOKY:

You love him? What do you mean? How? How do you love him?

CREATURE:

I love him.

SPOOKY:

Lord have mercy on Wasaychigan Hill!

CREATURE:

Rising suddenly.

I love the way he stands. I love the way he walks. The way he laughs. The way he wears his cowboy boots...

SPOOKY:

You're kidding me.

CREATURE:

...the way his tight blue jeans fall over his ass. The way he talks so smart and tough. The way women fall at his feet. I wanna be like him. I always wanted to be like him, William. I always wanted to have a dick as big as his.

SPOOKY:

Creature Alphonse Nataways? You know not what you say.

CREATURE:

I don't care.

SPOOKY:

I care.

CREATURE:

I don't care. I can't stand it anymore.

SPOOKY:

Shut up. You're making me nervous. Real nervous.

CREATURE:

Come with me.

SPOOKY:

Come with you where?

CREATURE:

To his house.

SPOOKY:

Who's house?

CREATURE:

Big Joey.

SPOOKY:

Are you crazy?

CREATURE:

Come with me.

SPOOKY:

No.

CREATURE:

Yes.

SPOOKY:

No.

CREATURE:

Suddenly and viciously grabbing Spooky by the throat.
Cut the goddamn bull crap, Spooky Lacroix!
Spooky tries desperately to save the christening gown.
I seen you crawl in the mud and shit so drunk you were
snortin' like a pig.

SPOOKY:

I changed my ways, thank you.

CREATURE:

Twenty one years. Twenty one years ago. You, me, Big Joey, Eugene Starblanket, that goddamn Zachary Jeremiah Keechigeesik. We were eighteen. We cut our wrists. Your own father's huntin' knife. We mixed blood. Swore we'd be friends for life. Frontenac Hotel. Twenty one years ago. You got jumped by seven white guys. Broken beer bottle come straight at your face. If it wasn't for me, you wouldn't be here today, wavin' that stinkin' bible in my face like it was a slab of meat. I'm not a dog. I'm your buddy. Your friend.

SPOOKY:

I know that.

Creature tightens his hold on Spooky's throat. The two men are staring straight into each other's eyes, inches apart. Silence.

CREATURE:

William. Think of your father. Remember the words of Nicotine Lacroix.

Long pause.

"Men who do not worship the Christian way do not automatically go to hell. There are many, many other ways of communicating with the Great Spirit. And they are all perfectly legitimate. What them priests said about me—about us—is not right. It's just not right. Respect us. Respect all people!" Remember that?

Long pause. Finally, Spooky screams, throwing the christening gown, knitting needles and all, over the bible on the table.

SPOOKY:

You goddamn, fucking son-of-a-bitch!

Black-out. Gunshots in the distance.

Lights up on Big Joey's living room/kitchen. Big Joey is sitting, silent and motionless, on the couch, staring straight ahead, as though he were in a trance. His hunting rifle rests on his lap. Dickie Bird Halked stands directly in front of and facing the life-size pin-up poster of Marilyn Monroe, also as though he were in a trance. Then his head drops down in remorse. Big Joey lifts the gun, loads it and aims it out directly in front. When Dickie Bird hears the snap of the gun being loaded, he turns to look. Then he slowly walks over to Big Joey, kneels down directly in front of the barrel of the gun, puts it in his mouth and then slowly reaches over and gently, almost lovingly, moves Big Joey's hand away from the trigger, caressing the older man's hand as he does. Big Joey slowly looks up at Dickie Bird's face, stunned. Dickie Bird puts his own thumb on the trigger and pulls. Click. Nothing. In the complete silence, the two men are looking directly into each other's eyes. Complete stillness. Fade-out. Split seconds before complete black-out, Marilyn Monroe farts, courtesy of Ms. Nanabush: a little flag reading "poot" pops up out of Ms. Monroe's derriere, as on a play gun. We hear a cute little "poot" sound.

Out of this black-out emerges the sound of a harmonica; it is Zachary Jeremiah Keechigeesik playing his heart out. Fade-in on Pierre St. Pierre, still in his night-clothes but also wearing his winter coat and hat over them, rushing all over the "forest" ostensibly rushing to Big Joey's house to warn Dickie Bird Halked about the gun-toting Simon Starblanket. He mutters to himself as he goes.

PIERRE:
...Hockey. Life. Hockey. Life. Hockey. Life...
Zachary appears in the shadows and sees Pierre.
ZACHARY:
Hey!
PIERRE:
Not hearing Zachary.
...Hockey. Life. Hockey. Life...

ZACHARY:
Pssst!
PIERRE:
Still not hearing Zachary.
...Hockey. Life. Hockey. Life.
Pause.
Hockey life!
ZACHARY:
Finally yelling.
Pierre St. Pierre!
Pierre jumps.
PIERRE:
Hallelujah! Have you heard the news?
ZACHARY:
The Band Council went and okayed Big Joey's radio
station.
PIERRE:
All the Indian women in the world is playin' hockey
now! World Hockey League, they call themselves.
Aboriginal Women's WHL. My wife, Veronique St.
Pierre, she just got the news. Eegeeweetamagoot fax
machine. ("Fax machine told her.") It's like a burnin',
ragin', blindin' fever out there. Them Cree women in
Saskatchewan, them Blood women in Alberta, them
Yakima, them Heidis out in the middle of your Spe-
cific Ocean, them Kickapoo, Chickasaw, Cherokee,
Chipewyan, Choctaw, Chippewa, Wichita, Kiowa down
in Oklahoma, them Seminole, Navajo, Onondaga,
Tuscarora, Winnebago, Mimac-paddy-wack-why-it's-
enough-to-give-your-dog-a-bone!...
*As, getting completely carried away, he grabs his
crotch.*
ZACHARY:
Pierre. Pierre.

PIERRE:

...they're turnin' the whole world topsy-turkey right before our very eyes and the Prime Minister's a-shittin' grape juice...

A gunshot explodes in the near distance. Pierre suddenly lays low and changes tone completely.

Holy shit la marde! He's after Dickie Bird. There's a red-eyed, crazed devil out there and he's after Dickie Bird Halked and he's gonna kill us all if we don't stop him right this minute.

ZACHARY:

Who? Who's gonna kill us?

PIERRE:

Simon Starblanket. Drunk. Power mad. Half-crazed on whiskey and he's got a gun.

ZACHARY:

Simon?

PIERRE:

He's drunk and he's mean and he's out to kill.

Another gunshot.

Hear that?

ZACHARY:

To himself.

That's Simon? I thought...

PIERRE:

When he heard about the Pegahmagahbow rape...

ZACHARY:

Pegahmagahbow what?

PIERRE:

Why, haven't you heard? Dickie Bird Halked raped Patsy Pegahmagahbow in most brutal fashion and Simon Starblanket is out to kill Dickie Bird Halked so I'm on my way to Big Joey's right this minute and I'm takin' that huntin' rifle of his and I'm sittin' next to that Halked boy right up until the cows come home.

Exits.
ZACHARY:
To himself.
Simon Starblanket. Patsy...
Black-out.

Out of this black-out come the gunshots, much louder this time, and Simon's wailing voice.
SIMON:
Aieeeeee-yip-yip! Nanabush!...
Fade-in on Simon, in the forest close by the large rock, still carrying his hunting rifle. Simon is half-crazed by this time, drunk out of his skull. The full moon glows.
...Weesageechak! Come back! Rosie! Rosie Kakapetum, tell him to come back, not to run away, cuz we need him...
Nanabush/Patsy Pegahmagahbow's voice comes filtering out of the darkness on the upper level. It is as though Simon were hearing a voice from inside his head.
NANABUSH/PATSY:
...her...
SIMON:
...him...
NANABUSH/PATSY:
...her...
Slow fade-in on Nanabush/Patsy, standing on the upper level, looking down at Simon. She still wears her very large bum.
SIMON:
...weetha ("him/her" — i.e., no gender) ... Christ! What is it? Him? Her? Stupid fucking language, fuck you, da Englesa. Me no speakum no more da goodie

Englesa, in Cree we say "weetha," not "him" or "her"
Nanabush, come back!
*Speaks directly to Nanabush, as though he/she were
there, directly in front of him; he doesn't see Nanabush/
Patsy standing on the upper level.*
Aw, boozhoo how are ya? Me good. Me berry, berry
good. I seen you! I just seen you jumping jack-ass thisa
away...
NANABUSH/PATSY:
*As though she/he were playing games behind Simon's
back.*
...and thataway...
SIMON:
...and thisaway and...
NANABUSH/PATSY:
...thataway...
SIMON:
...and thisaway and...
NANABUSH/PATSY:
...thataway...
SIMON:
...and thisaway and...
NANABUSH/PATSY:
...thataway...
SIMON:
...etcetra, etcetra, etcetra...
NANABUSH/PATSY:
...etcetERA.
Pause.
She's here! She's here!
SIMON:
...Nanabush! Weesageechak!...
*Nanabush/Patsy peals out with a silvery, magical
laugh that echoes and echoes.*

...Dey shove dis...whach-you-ma-call-it...da crucifix up your holy cunt ouch, eh? Ouch, eh?
Simon sees the bloody crucifix sitting on the rock and slowly approaches it. He kneels directly before it.
Nah...
Laughs a long mad, hysterical laugh that ends with hysterical weeping.
...yessssss...noooo...oh, noooo! Crucifix!
Spits violently on the crucifix.
Fucking goddamn crucifix yesssss... God! You're a man. You're a woman. You're a man? You're a woman? You see, nineethoowan poogoo neetha ("I speak only Cree")...

NANABUSH/PATSY:
...ohhh...

SIMON:
...keetha ma-a? ("How about you?")... Nah. Da Englesa him...

NANABUSH/PATSY:
...her...

SIMON:
...him...

NANABUSH/PATSY:
...her...

SIMON:
...him!...

NANABUSH/PATSY:
...her!...

SIMON:
...all da time...

NANABUSH/PATSY:
...all da time...

SIMON:
...tsk, tsk, tsk...

NANABUSH/PATSY:

...tsk, tsk, tsk.

SIMON:

If God, you are a woman/man in Cree but only a man in da Englesa, then how come you still got a cun...

NANABUSH/PATSY:

...a womb.

With this, Simon finally sees Nanabush/Patsy. He calls out to her.

SIMON:

Patsy! Big Bum Pegahmagahbow, you flying across da ice on world's biggest puck. Patsy, look what dey done to your puss...

Nanabush/Patsy lifts her skirt and displays the blood stain on her panties. She then finally takes off the prosthetic that is her huge bum and holds it in one arm.

Hey!

And Nanabush/Patsy holds an eagle feather up in the air, ready to dance. Simon stomps on the ground, rhythmically, and sings.

"...and me I don't wanna go to the moon, I'm gonna leave that moon alone. I just wanna dance with the Rosebud Sioux this summer, yeah, yeah, yeah..."

Simon chants and he and Nanabush/Patsy dance, he on the lower level with his hunting rifle in the air, she on the upper level with her eagle feather.

How, astum, Patsy, kiam. N'tayneemeetootan. ("Come on, Patsy, never mind. Let's go dance.")

We hear Zachary Jeremiah Keechigeesik's voice calling from the darkness a distance away.

ZACHARY:

Hey!

But Simon and Nanabush/Patsy pay no heed.

NANABUSH/PATSY:
...n'tayneemeetootan South Dakota?...
SIMON:
...how, astum, Patsy. N'tayneemeetootan South Dakota.
Hey, Patsy Pegahmagahbow....
As he finally approaches her and holds his hand out.
NANABUSH/PATSY:
As she holds her hand out toward his.
...Simon Starblanket...
SIMON/NANABUSH/PATSY:
...eenpaysagee-itan ("I love you to death") ...
Zachary finally emerges tentatively from the shadows. He is holding a beautiful, fresh pie. Nanabush/ Patsy disappears.
ZACHARY:
Calling out over the distance.
Hey! You want some pie?
SIMON:
Silence. Calling back.
What?!
Not seeing Zachary, he looks around cautiously.
ZACHARY:
I said. You want some pie?
SIMON:
Calling back, after some confused thought.
What?
ZACHARY:
He approaches Simon slowly.
Do you want some pie?
SIMON:
Silence. Finally, he sees Zachary and points the gun at him.
What kind?

ZACHARY:
Apple. I just made some. It's still hot.
SIMON:
Long pause.
Okay.
Slowly, Nanabush/Patsy enters the scene and comes up behind Simon, holding Simon's dancing bustle in front of her, as in a ceremony.
ZACHARY:
Okay. But you gotta give me the gun first.
The gun goes off accidentally, just missing Zachary's head.
I said, you gotta give me the gun first.
Gradually, the dancing bustle begins to shimmer and dance in Nanabush/Patsy's hands.
SIMON:
Patsy. I gotta go see Patsy.
ZACHARY:
You and me and Patsy and Hera. We're gonna go have some pie. Fresh, hot apple pie. Then, we go to Sudbury and have a look at that Mobart, what do you say?
The shimmering movements of the bustle balloon out into these magical, dance-like arches, as Nanabush/ Patsy maneuvers it directly in front of Simon, hiding him momentarily. Behind this, Simon drops the base of the rifle to the ground, causing it to go off accidentally. The bullet hits Simon in the stomach. He falls to the ground. Zachary lets go of his pie and runs over to him. The shimmering of the bustle dies off into the darkness of the forest and disappears, Nanabush/ Patsy maneuvering it.
ZACHARY:
Simon! Simon! Oh, lordy, lordy, lordy... Are you alright? Are you okay? Simon. Simon. Talk to me.

Goodness sakes, talk to me Simon. Ayumi-in! ("Talk to me!")

SIMON:

Barely able to speak, as he sinks slowly to the ground beside the large rock.

Kamoowanow...apple...pie...patima...neetha...igwa Patsy...n'gapeetootanan...patima..apple...pie...neee. ("We'll eat...apple...pie...later...me...and Patsy...we'll come over...later...apple...pie...neee.")

He dies.

ZACHARY:

As he kneels over Simon's body, the full moon glowing even redder.

Oh, lordy, lordy... Holy shit! Holy shit! What's happening? What's become of this place? What's happening to this place? What's happening to these people? My people. He didn't have to die. He didn't have to die. That's the goddamn most stupid...no reason...this kind of living has got to stop. It's got to stop!

Talking and then just shrieking at the sky.

Aieeeeeee-Lord! God! God of the Indian! God of the Whiteman! God-Al-fucking-mighty! Whatever the fuck your name is. Why are you doing this to us? Why are you doing this to us? Are you up there at all? Or are you some stupid, drunken shit, out-of-your-mind-passed out under some great beer table up there in your stupid fucking clouds? Come down! Astum oota! ("Come down here!") Why don't you come down? I dare you to come down from your high-falutin' fuckin' shit-throne up there, come down and show us you got the guts to stop this stupid, stupid, stupid way of living. It's got to stop. It's got to stop. It's got to stop. It's got to stop. It's got to stop. It's got to stop...

He collapses over Simon's body and weeps. Fade-out.

Towards the end of this speech, a light comes up on Nanabush. Her perch (i.e., the jukebox) has swivelled around and she is sitting on a toilet having a good shit. He/she is dressed in an old man's white beard and wig, but also wearing sexy, elegant women's high-heeled pumps. Surrounded by white, puffy clouds, she/he sits with her legs crossed, nonchalantly filing his/her fingernails. Fade-out.

Fade-in on Big Joey's living room/kitchen. Big Joey, Dickie Bird Halked, Creature Nataways, Spooky Lacroix and Pierre St. Pierre are sitting and standing in various positions, in complete silence. A hush pervades the room for about twenty beats. Dickie Bird is holding Big Joey's hunting rifle. Suddenly, Zachary Jeremiah Keechigeesik enters, in a semi-crazed state. Dickie Bird starts and points the rifle straight at Zachary's head.

CREATURE:
Zachary Jeremiah! What are you doing here?

BIG JOEY:
Lookin' for your shorts, Zach?
From his position on the couch, he motions Dickie Bird to put the gun down. Dickie Bird does so.

ZACHARY:
To Big Joey.
You're unbelievable. You're fucking unbelievable. You let this young man, you let your own son get away with this inconceivable act...

CREATURE:
Don't say that to him, Zachary Jeremiah, don't say that...

ZACHARY:
Ignoring Creature.

You know he did it and you're hiding him what in God's name is wrong with you?

SPOOKY:

Zachary Jeremiah, you're not yourself...

PIERRE:

Nope. Not himself. Talkin' wild.

Sensing potential violence, he sneaks out the door.

BIG JOEY:

To Zachary.

He don't even know he done anything.

ZACHARY:

Bull shit! They're not even sure the air ambulance will get Patsy Pegahmagahbow to Sudbury in time. Simon Starblanket just shot himself and this boy is responsible...

Simon rises slowly from the ground and "sleep walks" right through this scene and up to the upper level, towards the full moon. The men are only vaguely aware of his passing.

BIG JOEY:

He ain't responsible for nothin'.

ZACHARY:

Simon Starblanket was on his way to South Dakota where he could have learned a few things and made something of himself, same place you went and made a total asshole of yourself seventeen years ago...

CREATURE:

Shush, Zachary Jeremiah, that's the past...

SPOOKY:

...the past...

CREATURE:

...Chris'sakes...

ZACHARY:

What happened to all those dreams you were so full of

for your people, the same dreams this young man just
died for?

SPOOKY:

To Big Joey, though not looking at him.

And my sister, Black Lady Halked, seventeen years ago
at that bar, Big Joey, you could have stopped her
drinking, you could have sent her home and this thing
never would have happened. That was your son inside
her belly.

CREATURE:

He didn't do nothing. He wouldn't let me do nothing.
He just stood there and watched the whole thing...

SPOOKY:

Creature Nataways!

CREATURE:

I don't care. I'm gonna tell. He watched this little
bastard do that to Patsy Pegahmagahbow...

BIG JOEY:

Suddenly turning on Creature.

You little cocksucker!

*Dickie Bird hits Creature on the back with the butt
of the rifle, knocking him unconscious.*

SPOOKY:

Why, Big Joey, why did you do that?

Silence.

ZACHARY:

Yes, Joe. Why?

Long silence. All the men look at Big Joey.

BIG JOEY:

Raising his arms, as for a battle cry.

"This is the end of the suffering of a great nation!" That
was me. Wounded Knee, South Dakota, Spring of '73.
The FBI. They beat us to the ground. Again and again
and again. Ever since that spring, I've had these dreams

where blood is spillin' out from my groin, nothin' there
but blood and emptiness. It's like...I lost myself. So
when I saw this baby comin' out of Caroline, Black
Lady...Gazelle dancin'...all this blood...and I knew it
was gonna come...I...I tried to stop it... I freaked out. I
don't know what I did...and I knew it was mine...

ZACHARY:
Why? Why did you let him do it? Why? Why did you let
him do it? Why? Why did you let him do it? Why? Why
did you let him do it?
Finally grabbing Big Joey by the collar.
Why?! Why did you let him do it?!

BIG JOEY:
Breaking free from Zachary's hold.
Because I hate them! I hate them fuckin' bitches. Because they — our own women — took the fuckin'
power away from us faster than the FBI ever did.

SPOOKY:
Softly, in the background.
They always had it.
Silence.

BIG JOEY:
There. I said it. I'm tired. Tired.
He slumps down on the couch and cries.

ZACHARY:
Softly.
Joe. Joe.
Fade-out.

*Out of this darkness emerges the sound of Simon Star-
blanket's chanting voice. Away up over Nanabush's
perch, the moon begins to glow, fully and magnifi-
cently. Against it, in silhouette, we see Simon, wearing his powwow bustle. Simon Starblanket is dancing in the moon. Fade-out.*

Fade-in on the "ice" at the hockey arena, where Pierre St. Pierre, in full referee regalia, is gossiping with Creature Nataways and Spooky Lacroix. Creature is knitting, with great difficulty, pink baby booties. Spooky is holding his new baby, wrapped in a pale blue knit blanket. We hear the sound of a hockey arena, just before a big game.

PIERRE:

...she says to me: "did you know, Pierre St. Pierre, that Gazelle Nataways found Zachary Jeremiah Keechigeesik's undershorts under her chesterfield and washed them and put them in a box real nice, all folded up and even sprinkled her perfume all over them and sashayed herself over to Hera Keechigeesik's house and handed the box over to her? I just about had a heart attack," she says to me. "And what's more," she says to me, "when Hera Keechigeesik opened that box, there was a picture sittin' on top of them shorts, a color picture of none other than our very own Zachary Jeremiah Keechigeesik...

Unseen by Pierre, Zachary approaches the group, wearing a baker's hat and carrying a rolling pin.

...wearin' nothin' but the suit God gave him. That's when Hera Keechigeesik went wild, like a banshee tigger, and she tore the hair out of Gazelle Nataways which, as it turns out, was a wig..." Imagine. After all these years. "...and she beat Gazelle Nataways to a cinder, right there into the treacherous icy door-step. And that's when 'the particular puck' finally came squishin' out of them considerable Nataways bosoms." And gentlemen? The Wasy Wailerettes are on again!

CREATURE:

Ho-leee!

SPOOKY:

Holy fuck!

PIERRE:

And I say shit la ma...

Finally seeing Zachary, who is standing there, listening to all this.

...oh my...

Pierre turns quickly to Spooky's baby.

...hello there, koochie-koochie-koo, welcome to the world!

SPOOKY:

It's not koochie-koochie-koo, Pierre St. Pierre. Her name's "Kichigeechacha." Rhymes with Lalala. Ain't she purdy?

Up in the "bleachers," Big Joey enters and prepares his microphone stand. Dickie Bird enters with a big sign saying: "WASY-FM" and hangs it proudly up above the microphone stand.

PIERRE:

Aw, she'll be readin' that ole holy bible before you can go: "Phhht! Phhht!"

Pierre accidentally spits in the baby's face. Spooky shoos him away.

SPOOKY:

"Phhht! Phhht!" to you too, Pierre St. Pierre.

CREATURE:

Spooky Lacroix. Lalala. They never made it to Sudbury General.

SPOOKY:

I was busy helping Eugene Starblanket out with Simon...

SPOOKY/PIERRE:

...may he rest in peace...

ZACHARY:

Good old Rosie Kakapetum. "Stand and deliver," they said to her. And stand and deliver she did. How's the knitting going there, Creature Nataways?

CREATURE:

Kichigeechacha, my god-daughter, she's wearin' all the wrong colors. I gotta work like a dog.

PIERRE:

Calling up to Dickie Bird Halked.

Don't you worry a wart about that court appearance, Dickie Bird Halked. I'll be right there beside you tellin' that ole judge a thing or two about that goddamn jukebox.

SPOOKY:

To Creature.

Come on. Let's go watch Lalala play her first game.

He and Creature go up to the "bleachers" on the upper level, directly in front of Nanabush's perch, to watch the big "game."

PIERRE:

Reading from his clip-board and checking off the list.

Now then, Dominique Ladouche, Black Lady Halked, Annie Cook, June Bug McLeod...

He stops abruptly for Big Joey's announcement, as do the other men.

BIG JOEY:

On the microphone.

Patsy Pegahmagahbow, who is recuperating at Sudbury General Hospital, sends her love and requests that the first goal scored by the Wasy Wailerettes be dedicated to the memory of Simon Starblanket...

Creature and Spooky, with knitting and baby, respectively, are now up in the "bleachers" with Dickie Bird and Big Joey, who are standing beside each other *at the microphone stand. Pierre St. Pierre is again skating around on the "ice" in his own inimitable fashion, "warming up." Zachary Jeremiah Keechigeesik, meanwhile, now has his apple pie, as well as his rolling pin, in hand, still wearing his baker's hat. At this point, the hockey arena sounds shift abruptly to the sound of women wailing and pucks hitting boards, echoing and echoing as in a vast empty chamber. As this "hockey game sequence" progresses, the spectacle of the men watching, cheering, etc., becomes more and more dream-like, all the men's movements imperceptibly breaking down into slow motion, until they fade, later, into the darkness. Zachary "sleep walks" through the whole lower level of the set, almost as though he were retracing his steps back through the whole play. Slowly, he takes off his clothes item by item, until, by the end, he is back lying naked on the couch where he began the play, except that, this time, it will be his own couch he is lying on. Big Joey continues uninterrupted:**

...And there they are, ladies igwa gentlemen, there they are, the most beautiful, daring, death-defying Indian women in the world, the Wasy Wailerettes! How, Number Nine Hera Keechigeesik, CAPTAIN of the Wasy Wailerettes, face-off igwa itootum asichi Number Nine Flora McDonald, Captain of the Canoe Laker Bravettes. Hey, soogi pagichee-ipinew "particular puck" referee Pierre St. Pierre...

CREATURE:
Go Hera go! Go Hera go! Go Hera go!...
Repeated all the way through — and under — Big Joey's commentary.

---

* the following hockey commentary by Big Joey (pages 124-126) is translated on pages 133-134.

BIG JOEY:
...igwa seemak wathay g'waskootoo like a herd of wild turtles...

SPOOKY:
Wasy once. Wasy twice. Holy jumping Jesus Christ! Rim ram. God damn. Fuck, son-of-a-bitch, shit!
Repeated in time to Creature's cheer, all the way through — and under — Big Joey's commentary.

BIG JOEY:
...Hey, aspin Number Six Dry Lips Manigitogan, right-winger for the Wasy Wailerettes, eemaskamat Number Thirteen of the Canoe Lake Bravettes anee-i "particular puck"...
Dickie Bird begins chanting and stomping his foot in time to Creature's and Spooky's cheers. Bits and pieces of Nanabush/Gazelle Nataways' "strip music" and Kitty Wells' "It Wasn't God Who Made Honky Tonk Angels" begin to weave in and out of this "sound collage," a collage which now has a definite "pounding" rhythm to it. Over it all soars the sound of Zachary's harmonica, swooping and diving brilliantly, recalling many of Nanabush's appearances throughout the play. Big Joey continues uninterrupted.

BIG JOEY:
...igwa aspin sipweesinskwataygew. Hey, k'seegoochin! How, Number Six Dry Lips Manigitogan igwa soogi pugamawew anee-i "particular puck" ita Number Twenty-six Little Girl Manitowabi, left-winger for the Wasy Wailerettes, katee-ooteetuk blue line ita Number Eleven Black Lady Halked, wha! defense-woman for the Wasy Wailerettes, kagatchitnat anee-i "particular puck" igwa seemak kapassiwatat Captain Hera Keechigeesikwa igwa Hera Keechigeesik mitooni eepimithat, hey, kwayus graceful Hera Keechigeesik, mitooni Russian ballerina eesinagoosit. Captain Hera

Keechigeesik bee-line igwa itootum straight for the
Canoe Lake Bravettes' net igwa shootiwatew anee-i
"particular puck" igwa she shoots, she scores...almost!
Wha! Close one, ladies igwa gentlemen, kwayus close
one. But Number Six Dry Lips Manigitogan, right-win-
ger for the Wasy Wailerettes, accidentally tripped and
blocked the shot...
Big Joey's voice begins to trail off as, at this point,
Creature Nataways marches over and angrily grabs
the microphone away from him.
...How, Number Nine Flora McDonald, Captain of the
Canoe Lake Bravettes, igwa ooteetinew anee-i "par-
ticular puck" igwa skate-oo-oo behind the net igwa
soogi heading along the right side of the rink ita
Number Twenty-one Annie Cook...
CREATURE:
Off microphone, as he marches over to it.
Aw shit! Aw shit!...
He grabs the microphone and, as he talks into it, the
sound of all the other men's voices, including the
entire "sound collage", begins to fade.
...That Dry Lips Manigitogan, she's no damn good,
Spooky Lacroix, I tole you once I tole you twice she
shouldna done it she shouldna done what she went and
did goddawful Dry Lips Manigitogan they shouldna let
her play, she's too fat, she's gotten positively blubbery
lately, I tole you once I tole you twice that Dry Lips
Manigitogan oughta move to Kapuskasing, she really
oughta, Spooky Lacroix. I tole you once I tole you
twice she oughta move to Kapuskasing, Dry Lips
oughta move to Kapuskasing! Dry Lips oughta move to
Kapuskasing! Dry Lips oughta move to Kapuskasing!
Dry Lips oughta move to Kapuskasing Dry Lips oughta
move to Kapuskasing Dry Lips oughta move to Ka-

puskasing Dry Lips oughta move to Kapuskasing Dry
Lips oughta move to Kapuskasing Dry Lips oughta
move to Kapuskasing...

*And this, too, fades into, first a whisper, magnified on
tape to "other-wordly" proportions, then into a slow
kind of heavy breathing. On top of this we hear
Spooky's baby crying. Complete fade-out on all this
(lights and sound), except for the baby's crying and
the heavy breathing, which continue in the darkness.
When the lights come up again, we are in Zachary's
own living room (i.e., what was all along Big Joey's
living room/kitchen, only much cleaner). The couch
Zachary lies on is now covered with a "starblanket"
and over the pin-up poster of Marilyn Monroe now
hangs what was, earlier on, Nanabush's large pow-
wow dancing bustle. The theme from "The Smurfs"
television show bleeds in. Zachary is lying on the
couch face down, naked, sleeping and snoring. The
television tn front of the couch comes on and "The
Smurfs" are playing merrily away. Zachary's wife,
the "real" Hera Keechigeesik, enters carrying their
baby, who is covered completely with a blanket.
Hera is soothing the crying baby.* ˏ

ZACHARY:
Talking in his sleep.
...Dry Lips...oughta move to...Kapus...

HERA:
Poosees.

ZACHARY:
...kasing...damn silliest thing I heard in my life...

HERA:
Honey.
Bends over the couch and kisses Zachary on the bum.

ZACHARY:
  ...goodness sakes, Hera, you just had a baby...
  Suddenly, he jumps up and falls off the couch.
  Simon!
HERA:
  Yoah! Keegatch igwa kipageecheep'skawinan. ("Yoah!
  You almost knocked us down.")
ZACHARY:
  Hera! Where's my shorts?!
HERA:
  Neee, kigipoochimeek awus-chayees. ("Neee, just a
  couple of inches past the rim of your ass-hole.")
ZACHARY:
  Neee, chimagideedoosh. ("Neee, you unfragrant kozy":
  Ojibway.)
  He struggles to a sitting position on the couch.
HERA:
  Correcting him and laughing.
  "ChimagideeDEESH." ("You unfragrant KOOZIE.")
ZACHARY:
  Alright. "ChimagideeDEESH."
HERA:
  And what were you dreaming abou...
ZACHARY:
  Finally seeing the television.
  Hey, it's the Smurfs! And they're not playing hockey da
  Englesa.
HERA:
  Neee, machi ma-a tatoo-Saturday morning Smurfs.
  Mootha meena weegatch hockey meetaweewuk
  weethawow Smurfs. ("Well, of course, the Smurfs are
  on every Saturday morning. But they never play hockey,
  those Smurfs.") Here, you take her.
  *She hands the baby over to Zachary and goes to sit
  beside him.*

Boy, that full moon last night. Ever look particularly like a giant puck, eh? Neee...
Silence. Zachary plays with the baby.
ZACHARY:
To Hera.
Hey, cup-cake. You ever think of playing hockey?
HERA:
Yeah, right. That's all I need is a flying puck right in the left tit, neee...
But she stops to speculate.
...hockey, hmmm...
ZACHARY:
To himself.
Lordy, lordy, lordy...
Hera fishes Zachary's undershorts, which are pale blue in color, from under a cushion and hands them to him. Zachary gladly grabs them.
Neee, magawa nipeetawitoos... ("Neee, here's my sharts...")
HERA:
Correcting him and laughing.
"NipeetawiTAS." ("My SHORTS.")
ZACHARY:
Alright. "NipeetawiTAS."
Dangles the shorts up to the baby's face with thumb and fore-finger and laughs. Sing-songy, bouncing the baby on his lap.
Magawa nipeetawitas. Oh yes, my little goddess, you've come back to me, haven't you, oh yes, magawa nipeetawitas...
Throws the shorts away and holds the baby with both hands, speaking right to her face, lovingly.
...Nipeetawitas. Nipeetawitas. Nipeetawitas, neee...
The baby finally gets "dislodged" from the blanket and emerges, naked. And the last thing we see is this

beautiful naked Indian man lifting this naked baby Indian girl up in the air, his wife sitting beside them watching and laughing. Slow fade-out. Split seconds before complete black-out, Hera peals out with this magical, silvery Nanabush laugh, which is echoed and echoed by one last magical arpeggio on the harmonica, from off-stage. Finally, in the darkness, the last sound we hear is the baby's laughing voice, magnified on tape to fill the entire theater. And this, too, fades into complete silence.

End of play.

Translation from the Cree of Big Joey's hockey commentary, Act One, pages 71-74.

...Hey, and there goes Number Six Dry Lips Manigitogan, right-winger for the Wasy Wailerettes...and steals the puck from Number Thirteen of the Canoe Lake Bravettes...and skates off. Hey, is she ever flying...
Off microphone.
Creature Nataways. Shut up.
To the other men
Get this asshole out of here.
Back on microphone.
Now, Number Six Dry Lips Manigitogan, right-winger for the Wasy Wailerettes, shoots the puck and the puck goes flying over towards the center-line...where Number Nine Hera Keechigeesik, left-winger for...the Wasy Wailerettes, catches it. Now, Number Nine Hera Keechigeesik...approaching the blue line where Number One Gazelle Nataways, Captain of the Wasy Wailerettes, tries to get the puck off her, but Number Nine Hera Keechigeesik won't give it to her. Wha! "Hooking," says referee Pierre St. Pierre, Gazelle Nataways has apparently hooked her own team-mate Hera Keechigeesik, wha! How, Number One Gazelle Nataways, Captain of the Wasy Wailerettes, facing off once

again with Number Nine Flora McDonald, Captain of
the Canoe Lake Bravettes and Flora McDonald shoots
the puck, but Number Thirty-seven Big Bum Pegahmagahbow, defense-woman for the Wasy Wailerettes,
stops the puck and passes it to Number Eleven Black
Lady Halked, also defense-woman for the Wasy Wailerettes, but Gazelle Nataways, Captain of the Wasy
Wailerettes, gives a mean body check to her own team-
mate Black Lady Halked woops! She falls, ladies and
gentlemen, Black Lady Halked hits the boards and
Black Lady Halked is singin' the blues, ladies and
gentlemen, Black Lady sings the blues.

Off microphone.

What the hell is going on down there? Dickie Bird, get
off the ice!

Back on microphone.

Wha! Number Eleven Black Lady Halked is up in a
flash and grabs the puck from Gazelle Nataways, holy
shit! The ailing but very, very furious Black Lady
Halked skates back, turns and takes aim, it's gonna be
a slap shot, ladies and gentlemen, Black Lady Halked
is gonna take a slap shot for sure and Black Lady
Halked shoots the puck, wha! She shoots straight at
her very own captain, Gazelle Nataways and holy shit,
holy shit, holy fuckin' shit!

Translation from the Cree of Big Joey's hockey commentary, Act Two, pages 124-126.

...And there they are, ladies and gentlemen, there they are, the most beautiful, daring, death-defying Indian women in the world, the Wasy Wailerettes! Now, Number Nine Hera Keechigeesik, CAPTAIN of the Wasy Wailerettes, facing off with Number Nine Flora McDonald, Captain of the Canoe Lake Bravettes. Hey, and referee Pierre St. Pierre drops the "particular puck"...and takes off like a herd of wild turtles...Hey, and there goes Dry Lips Manigitogan, right-winger for the Wasy Wailerettes, and steals the "particular puck" from Number Thirteen of the Canoe Lake Bravettes...and skates off. Hey, is she ever flying. Now, Number Six Dry Lips Manigitogan shoots the "particular puck" towards where Number Twenty-six Little Girl Manitowabi, left-winger for the Wasy Wailerettes, is heading straight for the blue line where Number Eleven Black Lady Halked, wha! defense-woman for the Wasy Wailerettes, catches the "particular puck" and straightway passes it to Captain Hera Keechigeesik and Hera Keechigeesik is just a-flyin', hey, is she graceful or what, that Hera Keechigeesik, she looks just like a Russian ballerina. Captain Hera Keechigeesik now makes a bee-line straight for the Canoe Lake Bravettes' net and shoots the "particular puck" and she shoots, she scores...almost! Wha! Close one, ladies and gentlemen, real close one. But Number Six Dry Lips Manitigotan, right-winger for the Wasy Wailerettes, accidentally tripped and blocked the shot...

Creature Nataways grabs the microphone away from Big Joey.

...How, Number Nine Flora McDonald, Captain of the Canoe Lake Bravettes, grabs the "particular puck" and skates behind the net and now heading along the right side of the rink where Number Twenty one Annie Cook...

Tomson Highway
is the author of, among other plays, *The Rez Sisters*, which
won the Dora Mavor Moore Award for Best New Play
of 1986/87 and became a smash hit across Canada, going on to the Edinburgh International Festival in 1988.
Dry Lips Oughta Move to Kapuskasing is a companion play
to *The Rez Sisters* and it won four Dora Mavor Moore
Awards, including one for the Best New Play of 1988/
89. Tomson Highway is from the Brochet Indian Reserve
in northern Manitoba but now lives in Toronto. Cree is
his first language.